UNDERSTANDING
WILLIAM KENNEDY

Understanding Contemporary
American Literature

Matthew J. Bruccoli, *Editor*

UNDERSTANDING
William
KENNEDY

J. K. VAN DOVER

UNIVERSITY OF SOUTH CAROLINA

Copyright © 1991 University of South Carolina

Published in Columbia, South Carolina, by the
University of South Carolina Press

Manufactured in the United States of America

Van Dover, J. Kenneth.
    Understanding William Kennedy / J.K. Van Dover.
        p. cm.—(Understanding contemporary American literature)
    Includes bibliographical references and index.
    ISBN 0-87249-663-5 (hard cover : acid free)
    1. Kennedy, William, 1928– —Criticism and interpretation.
I. Title. II. Series.
PS3561.E428Z9 1990
813′.54—dc20   90-28929

CONTENTS

For Lara and Andrew

EDITOR'S PREFACE

Understanding Contemporary American Literature has been planned as a series of guides or companions for students as well as good nonacademic readers. The editor and publisher perceive a need for these volumes because much of the influential contemporary literature makes special demands. Uninitiated readers encounter difficulty in approaching works that depart from the traditional forms and techniques of prose and poetry. Literature relies on conventions, but the conventions keep evolving; new writers form their own conventions—which in time may become familiar. Put simply, *UCAL* provides instruction in how to read certain contemporary writers—identifying and explicating their material, themes, use of language, point of view, structures, symbolism, and responses to experience.

The word *understanding* in the series title was deliberately chosen. Many willing readers lack an adequate understanding of how contemporary literature works; that is, what the author is attempting to express and the means by which it is conveyed. Although the criticism and analysis in the series have been aimed at a level of general accessibility, these introductory volumes are meant to be applied in conjunction with the works they cover. Thus they do not provide a substitute for the works and authors they introduce, but rather prepare the reader for more profitable literary experiences.

M. J. B.

UNDERSTANDING

WILLIAM KENNEDY

CHAPTER ONE

Understanding William Kennedy

Career

William Kennedy's life has already been fixed as a popular fable of the contemporary American literary scene—a fable of virtue finally rewarded. At age fifty-five, he could claim some success as an Albany journalist, but his career as a novelist had passed relatively unrewarded. His books had gone out of print, and his latest manuscript had been rejected by thirteen publishers. Then the Nobel Prize–winning novelist Saul Bellow intervened with the Viking Press, and that manuscript was published in 1983 as *Ironweed*. The book became a critically acclaimed best-seller. It won the National Book Critics Circle Award for Fiction and the Pulitzer Prize. His earlier novels were reprinted and reappraised. The MacArthur Foundation selected him for one of its generous five-year "genius" fellowships. He became a full professor at SUNY Albany, and he founded the Albany (later the New York State) Writer's Institute. He collaborated with Francis Ford Coppola on the screenplay of *The Cotton Club*. *Time* and *Newsweek* printed feature articles about him.

Albany declared a William Kennedy month. And, as un-deterred by fame as by obscurity, Kennedy continued to write, publishing his fifth novel, *Quinn's Book,* in 1988.

William Kennedy was born in Albany on 16 January 1928 to "a Catholic working-class family, Irish on all sides."[1] And Albany on all sides. A great-grandfather, "Big Jim" Carroll, was involved in Albany politics, and Kennedy's father was a county deputy sheriff for twenty-five years. His uncle Pete McDonald, in part the model for Billy Phelan, knew the nightlife of Albany in the 1920s and 30s, when Albany really had a nightlife. Kennedy was raised in an Irish neighborhood of north Albany, then rebelled against it—against "narrowback sermons" at Mass, against "Too-ra-loo-ra-loo-ra," against the Irish-Catholic Democratic machine which ran the town and the county. In mid-life, during a voluntary exile as a journalist in Puerto Rico, Kennedy realized that Albany was the inescapable location of his fiction: "I cared more about the shape of the ball returns in the Knights of Columbus alleys in Albany. . . . They were artifacts out of a significant past—my father's, my uncle's, my own—and San Juan had nothing comparable to offer."[2]

His Albany–Irish background comprises one of the defining elements of Kennedy's literary imagination. The second crucial factor influencing his approach to writing has been his career as a journalist. After graduating from Siena College, just north of Albany, in 1949, Kennedy began work as a sportswriter for the Glens Falls, New York, *Post Star.* He was drafted during the Korean War and assigned as a sportswriter to the Fourth Division in Europe. Upon his return to the States in 1952, he joined the staff of the Albany *Times-Union.* In 1956 he took a position with a short-lived English-language newspaper, the Puerto

Rico *World-Journal*. There he met his wife, Dana Sosa, a dancer and actress (the couple have three children, Dana, Kathy, and Brenden). He worked briefly for *The Miami Herald*, then returned to Puerto Rico as the managing editor of the San Juan *Star*. Finally in 1963 he returned to Albany and the *Times-Union*, where he worked in various capacities: muckraker, reviewer, columnist. In 1969 he published his first novel, *The Ink Truck*.

Kennedy has not been a prolific writer of fiction. His most recent novel, *Quinn's Book*, is his fifth. He has published only two short stories since the early pieces which he published in *The San Juan Review*, pieces which he now dismisses. He has produced an important nonfiction volume, *O Albany!* (1983), and he continues to write reviews and occasional essays. But it is upon his novels that his claims as an artist are based. His recreations of particular moments of the American experience—of the *Albany* experience—have established him as an important contemporary American writer.

Reading William Kennedy

Understanding William Kennedy's fiction may not seem a difficult task. Kennedy is not primarily interested in challenging the reader with linguistic puzzles; his prose betrays his journalistic background in the clarity with which it communicates its story to the reader. But it is not naïve prose; Kennedy is a conscious stylist, and his narratives employ a number of voices to express a surprisingly broad range of experience. A careless reading will miss much. The most interesting aspects of his fiction are those related to the development of themes and characters. His novels present specific moments of Albany experience as microcosms of American experience. Only by attending to the patterns of action and behavior that emerge in the novels can the reader comprehend Kennedy's serious criticism of life in America. And because all of his novels are located in the limited environment of Albany and often share common characters, it is especially important to observe those larger patterns which emerge through several related novels. The "Albany Trilogy" of *Legs, Billy Phelan's Greatest Game,* and *Ironweed* may have been a publisher's device to exploit the sudden fame of the third novel, but Kennedy's novels clearly do build upon one another. And since the inauguration of the Phelan–Quinn–Daugherty saga in *Billy Phelan's Greatest Game* (1978), Kennedy has devoted himself to producing a deliberate and coherent multivolume representation of the American experience.

It should be admitted at once that Kennedy's protagonists and narrators have invariably been men. Women appear largely in supporting roles—as wives and mistresses. Though fathers seem very important, mothers are usually absent. The expanded roles of Maud and Magdalena in *Quinn's Book* suggest that Kennedy is moving to include women as primary interpreters of reality, but his fiction remains primarily an expression of the masculine experience of surviving in America.

Kennedy has denied working out of a specifically Irish literary tradition. He admits to admiring Beckett, Joyce, and Yeats, but also acknowledges the influence of writers as diverse as Günter Grass, Albert Camus, Ralph Ellison, Graham Greene, and Saul Bellow.[3] Still, there is some point to placing him in an Irish-American tradition that includes the proletarian fiction of James T. Farrell (*Studs*

Lonigan), the political fiction of Edwin O'Connor (*The Last Hurrah*), and the underrated gangster and crime fiction of George V. Higgins (*The Friends of Eddie Coyle*). (It might be relevant to note that the Irish–American tradition must also include the sophisticated fiction of the Albany-Irish novelist Henry James, who certainly influenced Kennedy.) But although his protagonists are invariably Irish, neither their difficulties nor their responses to their difficulties are simply Irish. Kennedy's characters lead very Albany-Irish lives, but they also face basic issues of American life: the immigrant's experience, heroic greed and materialism, economic pressures (epitomized by the Great Depression), the confrontation between labor and capital, and the confrontation between individual integrity and political reality.

Kennedy's representation of the Irish-American experience of America has many dimensions, but these can profitably be considered under two thematic headings: *Location* and *Dislocation*. Kennedy's characters are always definitely located in a particular matrix of place, time, and society. But they also invariably find themselves in opposition to the forces which control that matrix; they are all in some sense alienated and rebellious. A third heading, *Style*, covers Kennedy's distinctive approach to representing the experience of his characters.

Location

A sense of place: "I think that if you leave out place, you leave out one of the principal ingredients of fiction. We are what we are because of place to some degree."[4] Kennedy has repeatedly emphasized his conviction that good fiction must locate itself concretely in space. "If you don't have a sense of where somebody comes from,

you don't know who they are, imaginatively speaking."[5]
Kennedy knows where his characters come from: Albany,
New York. All of his novels are set in Albany, though in
the first, *The Ink Truck,* the city is unnamed. In successive
novels the city becomes more and more a central presence. Legs Diamond, in Kennedy's second novel, comes
to Albany only at the end of his career. The Albany he
discovers in 1930 is exactly re-created, but the personality
of the famous gangster dominates the city and the narrative. The city dominates Billy Phelan in *Billy Phelan's
Greatest Game.* Its streets and neighborhoods; its buildings—bars, hotels, bowling alleys; above all, its politics—these things define the place Billy comes from, and
they define him. They will also define his father, Francis,
in *Ironweed,* and, though to a lesser degree, in *Quinn's
Book* they define Billy's brother-in-law's grandfather,
Daniel Quinn.

Kennedy's Albany may lack some of the resonance of
Joyce's Dublin or of Faulkner's Yoknapatawpha County; it
is in many respects an unexceptional mid-sized American
city; its population in 1940 (*Billy Phelan's Greatest Game*
and *Ironweed* are set in 1938) was 130,447. Though it
lacks the vast dimensions of the more common scenes of
American urban fiction, Albany contains on a moderate
scale many of the same elements. It has been touched by
the political, industrial, and intellectual revolutions of
American history: Roosevelt and Rockefeller, the Erie Canal, Melville and James—these are some of the names associated with Albany. And when, in the early 1960s,
Kennedy first conceived what he called "Idea for an Albany Fantasy," "the plot included such Albany characters
as Philip Schuyler, the great Revolutionary War general;
Martin H. Glynn, the Irish newspaper editor who became

governor; Aaron Burr, Alexander Hamilton and Gen. John Burgoyne; Herman Melville and Henry James,'' and others.[6]

But the ''Albany Fantasy'' was not realized, and these are not the names which Kennedy's fictional Albanians usually conjure with. Kennedy's Albanians are not consciously burdened by a mythology; they are not trying to awaken from a nightmare of history. To be located in Albany is, as Kennedy says in a slightly different context, to be ''centered squarely in the American and the human continuum.''[7] Most of Kennedy's characters belong to the lower classes of Albany society: workers, derelicts, petty (and not so petty) criminals—what Marxists label as the proletariat and the *lumpenproletariat*. Their Albany is a pedestrian American city, with all the hazards and opportunities of a typical American city.

There are, however, some special aspects of Kennedy's Albany. Many of them emerge in the context of Kennedy's celebration of his city's character in *O Albany!* but two should be mentioned here: Albany is an ethnic city, and it is a political city. Albany is an old city, dating to the mid-seventeenth century, and its modern shape has been molded by a succession of immigrations. It was originally founded as a Dutch trading post, and, as *Quinn's Book* illustrates, the Dutch hegemony lasted until long after the city had been transferred to the English in 1664. By the mid-nineteenth century, when the English (the Yankees, the WASPs) had taken control, the Erie Canal was bringing masses of Irish to (and through) Albany, and it is the twentieth-century descendants of these Irish who people Kennedy's novels. The other ethnic groups who came later to Albany in large numbers—the Germans, the blacks, and the Italians—play a minor role in the fiction.

Albany has been a political city since 1797, when it was made the capital of one of the nation's largest and most influential states. But Kennedy has very little to say about state or national politics. The politics of his fiction is local, Albany politics. And from the 1920s to the 1970s Albany was governed by a powerful Democratic machine headed by the WASP mayor, Erastus Corning, and controlled by the Irishman, Boss Dan O'Connell. A fictionalized version of this machine operates in the background of *Ironweed,* and is a central power in *Billy Phelan's Greatest Game.*

Finally, it should be noted that everything Kennedy has written is, in a sense, part of his "Albany Cycle." The only exceptions are the two early stories published in *The San Juan Review* and his reviews of fiction and film, and of these only the latter are significant. Edward C. Reilly has compiled a biography of nearly seventy book reviews by Kennedy published between 1964 and 1989 in journals such as *The New Republic, The National Observer, The New York Times Book Review,* and *Look.* Kennedy's cosmopolitan interests are reflected in these reviews of American, European, and Latin American writers. But the remainder of his fiction and nonfiction is exclusively Albanian in origin. Whether he writes a piece for *Esquire* about Jack Rosenstein, an actual Albany oyster-shucker, or a novel about Francis Phelan, an imagined Albany bum, Albany provides the primary matter upon which Kennedy's imagination works. *O Albany!* is as much a part of the "cycle" as *Ironweed.*

A sense of time: Kennedy's first novel, *The Ink Truck,* was set in Albany, but there are few details in the narrative to confirm the placement. Similarly, the novel is set in the decade in which it was composed, the 1960s, but there are few specific signs of the times. In his novels since *The Ink Truck,* however, the historical dimension has been explicit, and indeed constitutes one of the distinctive virtues of Kennedy's approach to fiction. His sense of place is contingent upon time. His novels re-create a succession of Albanies—the Albany of Jack Diamond, that of the late 1920s and early 1930s; the Albany of Billy and Francis Phelan, that of 1938; the Albany of Daniel Quinn, that of the 1850s and 1860s. Kennedy's characters and the place they inhabit are carefully crafted to reflect the historical reality of their period. Kennedy is not much interested in historical fiction of the sort composed by E. L. Doctorow, James Michener, or Gore Vidal. With the exception of *Legs,* his novels do not feature the lives of historical figures, either as protagonists or as peripheral figures; with the exception of *Quinn's Book,* his characters are not designed simply to embody historical developments; they do not debate the great questions of the day. Kennedy is devoted rather to exploring the pressures—economic, social, ideological—which the times impose upon ordinary people and the ways ordinary people respond to these pressures.

A sense of society: Place and time yield a particular social reality. Kennedy's depiction of that reality tends to focus upon two contexts: the family and politics. Family plays an increasingly crucial role in his imagination. Since *Billy Phelan's Greatest Game* he has clearly dedicated himself to using a hundred years in the history of a connected group of Albany-Irish-Catholic families— the Phelans, Daughertys, and Quinns—as the basis for his fiction. Admiring Faulkner's Compsons, Joyce's

Daedalus, and Salinger's Glasses, Kennedy has admitted the attraction of "works that carried people, not in any sequential way, through great leaps in time, maturity, and psychological transformation."[8] Kennedy's first, unpublished attempt at a large fiction was a manuscript entitled *The Angels and the Sparrows,* an Albany-Irish-Catholic family chronicle which now serves as the ur-saga for his fiction. *Billy Phelan's Greatest Game, Ironweed,* and *Quinn's Book* are all derived, with changes and revisions, from this family chronicle. The relationships between fathers and sons seem especially important in Kennedy's fiction.

Politics, in Kennedy's Albany is in some respects merely family writ large. The all-powerful political machine is run by a family, the McCalls (Kennedy's surrogates for the historical O'Connell family), from their home in their neighborhood. And it is run through personal connections and family ties: whom you know, and whom your parents knew, can determine your success or failure in the Albany of the McCalls; and the Phelans, Daughertys, and Quinns know the McCalls. Kennedy does not debate partisan ideologies in his fiction; the McCalls are certainly Democrats, but there is no indication of their liberal or conservative tendencies. Power, not philosophy, is the matter of politics in Albany.

Dislocation

Alienation: The most distinctive feature of Kennedy's fiction lies in his careful location of his characters in place, time, and society; the main action of all his novels concerns the reaction of his protagonists against the world in which they are located. They refuse to accept the direction which the world would impose upon their lives, and they rebel against the various embodiments of worldly authority which they encounter—business managements, political machines, legal systems, family relationships. Though they are rooted in their particular Albanies, Kennedy's heroes all manage to twist from mere vegetable uprightness. Bailey, Legs Diamond, Billy and Francis Phelan, and Daniel Quinn all turn in some degree against their world. The striker, the gangster, the gamester, the derelict, and the orphan become types of possible rebellion.

Kennedy's fiction tends to unfold as a dialectic between the forces which tie the protagonist to his Albany and those which drive him from it. The protagonist never really escapes his Albany, but the repetition of the conflict allows Kennedy to view and review the struggle between the individual's self-assertion and the inescapability of his past—his place, his time, and his society.

Surrealism: Kennedy identified a sense of place as one of the central ingredients of fiction. But he has been equally explicit in asserting that physical place does not completely account for man's experience of his world. ''I don't think you can talk about the life of the soul if you don't talk about surrealistic metaphysical elements.''[9] And his novels are always marked by at least occasional signs of the paranormal—omens, precognitions, dreams, ghosts, extended fantasies. This feature of his fiction has led to comparisons with that of the Latin American ''magical realists.'' Kennedy's protagonists find themselves located in metaphysical as well as physical Albanies: they must negotiate with mystical persistences of the past and mystical intimations of the future as well as with the immediate, practical problems of making it through the day.

Style

His sense of place is surely Kennedy's distinctive strength as a novelist, but, like all good writers, his first commitment is to the language through which he conveys his sense of place: "Language is the sine qua non. . . . Language as style, language or elegance, language as life itself. That's what I care about, more than anything else, and if it doesn't have that, forget it."[10] Kennedy's Albanies and his characters are, after all, the creations of Kennedy's words. And Kennedy's language is a versatile instrument, capable of describing the bizarre experiences of Bailey; the violence and the charisma of Legs Diamond; the hard Depression world of the Phelans; and the nineteenth-century picaresque experiences of Daniel Quinn.

The essential qualities of Kennedy's style lie in his special combination of a journalist's vision with that of the poet. The first gives his prose its objectivity and exactness. (It also provides him with a breadth of background: the reporter's objective and exact knowledge of Albany's people and places is comprehensive.) The second gives the prose its power to suggest the peculiar significance a scene has for a particular perceiver. The virtue of this style can be seen in a passage in which Kennedy uses a prosaic itinerary through the streets of Albany to evoke the special relationship between a person and his city. Billy Phelan walks down Broadway on the night of Thursday, 20 October 1938:

> There was Albany's river of bright white lights, the lights on in the Famous Lunch, still open, and the dark, smoky reds of Brockley's and Becker's neon tubes, and the tubes also shaping the point over the

door of the American Hotel, and the window of
Louie's pool room lit up, where somebody was still
getting some action, and the light on in the Waldorf
restaurant, where the pimps worked out of and where
you could get a baked apple right now if you needed
one, and the lights of the Cadillac Cafeteria with the
pretty great custard pie . . . [11]

The sentence continues as Billy sees other lights that
night—those of the Cadillac Hotel, the Monte Carlo,
Chief Humphrey's private detective office, Joe Man-
gione's rooms above his fruit store, the back of Red's bar-
bershop. The sequence is as precise as any in *Ulysses*.

But precision is not the main purpose of the passage.
Billy does more than see the physical lights which illuminate his physical path—the incandescent bulbs and neon
tubes. He *recognizes* the lights; he instantly associates
each light with some human connection—action in a pool
room, a custard pie, a detective working on a divorce
case, some of the guys playing blackjack. Billy, an unem-
ployed gambler, may own very little in Depression Albany, but he possesses the Broadway lit by these lights.
This is his world.

The "lights" passage is a lyrical gazetteer that extends
for three pages, demonstrating Billy's intimate knowledge
of nighttime Albany. And this knowledge has been bred in
the bone. As he sets out on his walk, Billy recalls rowing
down the same street twenty-five years ago in the flood of
1913, a six-year-old boy in a boat with the father, Francis,
who would abandon the family in 1916 (a photograph of
Broadway during the 1913 flood is included in *O Albany!*). Billy's possession of his Broadway is the gift of a
lifetime of experience, and the special recollection of his

father bears upon a major theme in the novel. The exact addresses and descriptions which give such a concrete quality to Kennedy's re-creations of Albanies past never merely serve verisimilitude; they are always occasions for some character to remember a significant element of his past or present life. The sights of Kennedy's Albany are always seen by a particular seer.

Later in the same novel Martin Daugherty drives with Patsy McCall through the streets of north Albany. The drive is functional: Patsy wants to get out of town to give Martin secret instructions regarding a ransom pay-off. But Martin notices the route and calls to mind a variety of connections. They pass a water filtration plant by the filled-in bed of the Erie Canal, and Martin remembers Francis Phelan running from Albany after killing a trolley scab with a stone. He also hears "echoes of long-dead voices of old North End canalers and lumber handlers" and envisions the forlorn immigrants refused entrance to Albany in the times of cholera[12] (this last a historical vision which Kennedy re-creates in *Quinn's Book*). Patsy also drives past the car barns from which the scab-bearing trolleys emerged, and Martin remembers the play his father wrote about Francis and the scab. They pass Wolfert's Roost, the golf club where, Martin recalls, he played golf with his own now alienated son. And as they drive on, memory itself becomes the topic of Martin's mental journey through Albany: "The car sped along Northern Boulevard, through a rush of memories now for Martin, who considered that on this day, or another very soon, he might be dead. All the history in his head would disappear, the way his father's history was fading into whiteness."[13] Martin's relationships with Francis Phelan, with his own son, and with his senile father are all important in the novel; the trip with Patsy McCall allows a sequence of Albany scenes to strike these chords of his experience.

Style also means that Kennedy gives his main characters individual voices, voices that embody a variety of imaginative responses to their experiences of Albany. Especially in *Legs, Billy Phelan's Greatest Game,* and *Ironweed,* Kennedy's proletarian characters speak a vernacular which sounds authentic. This is the way gangsters, gamesters, and bums of the 20s and 30s must really have spoken, yet it is clearly not artless transcription. And this artful verisimilitude in the dialogue and much of the description is complemented in each of these novels by moments of lyrical, often mystical awareness expressed in poetic language. Kennedy's style is a flexible instrument. (*The Ink Truck* and *Quinn's Book,* with their more hectic actions, rely less upon the spoken voice as an evocative tool; their mode—in dialogue and description—is essentially rhetorical.)

The ways Kennedy's protagonists conclude their adventures reveal their individual approaches to their individual lives. In each instance the words reflect the character's mental response to his experience. Francis Phelan's voice—"If they were on to him, well that's all she wrote. Katie bar the door. Too wet to plow. He'd head where it was warm, where he would never again have to run from men or weather"[14]—is different in tone and diction as well as in sentiment from that of his son—"If Billy had died that night, he'd have died a sucker. But the sucker got wised up and he ain't anywheres near heaven yet"[15]—and both voices differ greatly from that of the nineteenth-century Daniel Quinn: "Quinn would dwell on this and perceive that he himself had changed, that he was forever isolated into the minority, a paddynigger and an obsessive fool whose disgust was greater than its object, who was trying to justify in this world what was justifiable only in another cosmic sphere."[16] Francis's sense of his diminishing options expresses itself in deliberate clichés which suggest an almost carefree fatalism. Billy sounds the note of a cocky, street-wise young man who has learned a lesson, but who has more lessons to learn. And Quinn speaks as a self-conscious hero of a *Bildungsroman,* commenting rhetorically upon the universal meaning of his experience.

Of course, single voices do not necessarily define the narratives. *Billy Phelan's Greatest Game* alternates between Billy's perspective and the more educated sensibility of Martin Daugherty. Billy tends instinctively to view experience as a challenging present. His awareness of the past and the future tends to be occasional and haphazard. Martin, by contrast, is, by character and by circumstances of plot, given to frequent recollections of the resonant past and to speculations about the future. In *Ironweed* not only is Francis's voice complemented by that of his companion, Helen Archer, whose perspective defines the novel's fifth chapter, Francis's voice itself operates at two levels. The first is his conscious sense of the quality of his own experience, a sense which is naturally limited by Francis's character as an itinerant bum. The second level is the third-person voice which, as Kennedy discovered in creating it, is "this ineffable level of Francis Phelan's life, a level which he would never get to consciously, but which was there somehow."[17] There is often a subtle interplay between these two levels of Francis's response to his world. Kennedy observes that "Francis moves in and out of those flights sometimes in the same sentence."[18]

It is worth noting that language is of professional concern to several of Kennedy's protagonists. Indeed, all but one of his heroes pursue one of two vocations: games or words. Billy and Francis Phelan are the gamesmen; Bailey, Martin Daugherty, Daniel Quinn are journalists. More specifically, they are, like Kennedy himself, advocacy journalists, columnists who attempt to use words to alter their worlds. Marcus Gorman, as a lawyer and as the memorialist of Legs Diamond, is also a professional worker with words. Jack Diamond himself is the exception, but the hero of *Legs,* with his eloquence and his risk-taking, combines elements of both the wordsman and the gamesman.

An aspect of Kennedy's style which should not be overlooked derives from his long-standing interest in the cinema. As he was working on his first published novel, *The Ink Truck,* he was also serving as a movie critic for the Albany *Times-Union.*[19] His interest in film eventually led him to work on the screenplays of *The Cotton Club* (with Francis Ford Coppola) and *Ironweed.* In both instances, he became actively involved in the production of the films. (He has also written screenplays for *Legs* and *Billy Phelan's Greatest Game* and has expressed his continuing interest in undertaking cinematic projects.[20]

Although in his essay on the filming of *Ironweed* Kennedy explicitly distinguishes between the different possibilities inherent in the two different media,[21] his sense of scene and form (and, as well perhaps, his sense of dialogue) has been influenced by the cinema. He has specifically mentioned Bergman (*Wild Strawberries*) and Fellini (*8 1/2*) as important influences.[22] His original conception of *Legs* called for the novel to be narrated from the point of view of a documentary camera. And it is not surprising that some critics found a sequence of filmlike scenes in *Quinn's Book:* the completion of the final draft of the novel coincided almost exactly with the completion of the filming of *Ironweed.*

NOTES

1. Larry McCaffery and Sinda Gregory, "An Interview with William Kennedy," *Alive and Writing* (Urbana: University of Illinois Press, 1987) 157.

2. William Kennedy, *O Albany!* (New York: Viking, 1983): 4.

3. McCaffery and Gregory 159.

4. Kay Bonetti, "An Interview with William Kennedy," *The Missouri Review* 8 (1985): 78.

5. McCaffery and Gregory 156.

6. Stephen Salisbury, "William Kennedy's Moveable Feast," *Philadelphia Inquirer Magazine* 31 July 1988: 36.

7. *O Albany!* 7.

8. McCaffery and Gregory 167.

9. Bonetti 79.

10. Bonetti 78–79.

11. William Kennedy, *Billy Phelan's Greatest Game* (New York: Viking, 1978) 132.

12. *Billy Phelan's* 229.

13. *Billy Phelan's* 231.

14. William Kennedy, *Ironweed* (New York: Viking, 1983) 227.

15. *Billy Phelan's* 281.

16. William Kennedy, *Quinn's Book* (New York: Viking, 1988) 288.

17. Douglas R. Allen and Mona Simpson, "The Art of Fiction CXI William Kennedy," *The Paris Review* 112 (Winter 1989): 50.

18. Allen and Simpson 51.

19. David Thomson, "The Man Has Legs," *Film Comment* 21 (1985): 57.

20. Edward C. Reilly, "On an Averill Park Afternoon with William Kennedy," *The South Carolina Review* 21 (1989): 23.

21. See Kennedy, *The Making of Ironweed* (New York: Penguin, 1988).

22. McCaffery and Gregory 164.

CHAPTER TWO

O Albany!

Although *O Albany! Improbable City of Political Wizards, Fearless Ethnics, Spectacular Aristocrats, Splendid Nobodies, and Underrated Scoundrels* was published in 1983 as Kennedy's fifth book, its origins are contemporary with Kennedy's first novel, and it provides the best introduction to the essential place of Kennedy's fiction. In 1964, having returned to the Albany *Times-Union* as a part-time reporter, Kennedy began a series of articles on the city's neighborhoods. These, rewritten, became the basis of *O Albany!* The book provides a very personal survey of the history, topography, and sociology of the place which has inspired all of Kennedy's fiction. (Kennedy has also written the essay that accompanies the photographs of William Clift in *The Capitol in Albany*.)

And the spirit with which Kennedy approached *O Albany!* is the same as that with which he approached his fiction. Its essays are also an attempt to re-create the city as a "magical place." When Kennedy says that in writing them he was inspired by "the feeling of going back and being able to reconstitute a time that was lost but could be reimagined and reconstituted as literature,"[1] he might as well be talking of *Legs* or *Billy Phelan's Greatest Game*. When, in *Ironweed*, Francis Phelan returns to his home on North Third Street, twenty-two years after his flight from Albany, he finds in an attic trunk the vital relics of his life prior to his flight. The attic setting is described as "this aerie of reconstitutable time."[2] Whether the actor is William Kennedy, the journalist attempting to re-create the actual past, or Francis Phelan, the fictional bum attempting to recover his personal past, the reconstituting of a time and place—a particular Albany with its particular Albanians—has been a main motif of Kennedy's art, fictional and nonfictional.

O Albany! is also a good starting point for understanding William Kennedy insofar as it represents Kennedy the journalist at his best. Its prose is the lucid, entertaining prose of a writer who wants to inform and delight the common reader, using facts, anecdotes, and wit. "Journalism," Kennedy has said, "is a great training ground. I was served enormously well by it. No bailsbondsman, no lawyer, no politician, no bartender, no actor can enter into the variety of worlds that a journalist can."[3] His career as a journalist thus provided Kennedy with both a deep knowledge of his place—its physical and social environments—and the discipline of a reportorial style. In the end Kennedy had to go beyond journalism to reconstitute Albany as literature. His effort to describe Albany's derelicts in a nonfiction book, the unpublished *Lemon Weed*, had to be transformed into *Ironweed*: "I had to take it to a further dimension of the imagination, where journalism can't go—if it's honest."[4] But a journalistic vision, a vision operating at its best in *O Albany!* remains a central element of Kennedy's art.

In addition to Kennedy's personal portraits and insights,

O Albany! offers pictures and maps of the people and the places that are important in his city. The book is a useful reminder that Kennedy has been a professional Albany-watcher, not just an enthusiastic dilettante. His own experience of the city (extended vicariously through the experiences of his Albany-watching relatives) is certainly the first source of Kennedy's knowledge of the city, but as a journalist he conscientiously investigated and analyzed precisely those aspects of Albany—its history, its ethnic cultures, and its politics—that determine so much in the lives of his fictional protagonists. Kennedy has studied his city, and in *O Albany!* he lays out the results of his research.

The main parts of *O Albany!* naturally reflect the character of Kennedy's personal vision of the city. Part 1, "The Magical Places," defines his priorities. Chapter 1, "Albany as a State of Mind," describes his personal imaginative bond to the city: his discovery in Puerto Rico that the city provided "an inexhaustible context for the stories I planned to write."[5] He quickly reviews Albany's long history—the Dutch patroonship, the Erie Canal, the melting pot, the political business of the city—and concludes: "It is centered squarely in the American and the human continuum, a magical place where the past becomes visible if one is willing to track the multiple incarnations of the city's soul" (7). In his journalism and in his fiction Kennedy has been willing.

The remaining four chapters of "The Magical Place" elaborate upon the principal sources of magic. "Legacy from a Lady" evokes the Dutch past through the genteel experience of an old patrician lady, Huybertie Pruyn, who was born in 1877. Huybertie's ancestor, Brandt Aertsz van Slechtenhorst, had come to Albany by 1646 as the

Patroon's agent, a director of the demesne of Rensselaer-wyck. Interviewed by Kennedy in the 1960s, Huybertie was an elegant upper-class lady who still remembered another Dutch Albanian, Herman Melville. She represents the aristocratic thread in Albany's history, a thread which Kennedy picks up in *Quinn's Book*.

Union Station, the subject of the brief chapter "The Romance of the Oriflamme," does not play an important role in the life of Legs Diamond, though it is the starting point of Marcus Gorman's crucial involvement in the gangster's affairs. But its grand façade, now decayed, does recall Albany's past prestige and its central geographical location, the features which attracted Legs to the city after the involuntary termination of his activities in New York City. Kennedy has played an active role in preventing the demolition of Albany landmarks such as Union Station and the Kenmore Hotel (one of Diamond's favorite hangouts and the scene of the beginning and the end of *Legs*).

The heart of Kennedy's Albany is described in "North Albany: Crucible for a Childhood." This is the neighborhood of Kennedy's own youth, and the chapter evokes its personal associations. It is also the neighborhood from which the Phelans, Daughertys, and McCalls emerged in the 1930s. Kennedy's school, PS 20, is their alma mater too. The chapter's twenty pages provide an invaluable perspective on the "magical" environment that produced both Kennedy and his Irish-Catholic protagonists.

And if "North Albany" defines the ethnic neighborhood context of Kennedy's major novels, the final chapter of "The Magical Places"—"The Democrats Convene, or, One Man's Family"—sets the local political context. Boss Dan O'Connell is the "one man," the chairman of the Democratic Committee; he and his family controlled the machine which controlled the city from the early 1920s until his death in 1977. The chapter describes some of the extralegal means by which O'Connell maintained his grip on power, a power which affected the lives of the Kennedys and the Phelans and even, if Kennedy's speculations are correct, determined the fate of Legs Diamond.

Part 2 of *O Albany!* is entitled "The Neighborhoods"—that is, the *other* neighborhoods, the ones to which the North End Irish moved to, or played in, or avoided. Its ten chapters provide a comprehensive survey of Albany's districts as they were and as they are—Downtown, Capitol Hill, the Bowery, and others. Kennedy is especially interested in the evolutionary process as castes of immigrants arrive and the city expands in distinctive segments. He is not much interested in official history—city administrations, corporate developments. Rather, he presents the common people, often in their own voices, describing their own environments and the changes they have observed. And these, of course, are the dominant voices in his fiction: ordinary working men and women (or, often, would-be working men and women). Here in part 2 and in the four chapters of part 4, "Some of the People" (Jews, Italians, Germans, blacks), he offers an uncondescending engagement with representatives of the various ethnic groups who live and work in Albany.

Part 3 of *O Albany!*—"Nighttown"—is devoted to the Albany of the Prohibition 1920s and 1930s, the Albany of Legs Diamond and Billy Phelan. Two of the three chapters deal with the topics of gambling and drinking; the third specifically deals with "The Death of Legs Diamond." Here Kennedy updates the research that went into his 1975 novel, *Legs.* He advances the thesis that the assassins who finally put three bullets into the head of the legendary Legs were not, as commonly believed, rival gangsters, but in fact police officials acting on instructions from the O'Connell machine.

O Albany! culminates in part 5, "Long-Run Politics: Wizardry Unbound," Kennedy's portrait of the crucial political character of his city. (Part 6, "Closing Time," is composed of brief acknowledgments and farewells.) Two men dominate the scene: Boss Daniel O'Connell ("They Bury the Boss: Dan Ex-Machina") and Mayor Erastus Corning ("Erastus: The Million Dollar Smile"). The chapter on Boss Dan is especially useful as background to *Billy Phelan's Greatest Game,* in which Boss Patsy Mc-Call and his family are the unmistakable surrogates for Boss Daniel O'Connell and his family. Between them, O'Connell and Corning ran the city and the county of Albany for more than fifty years. Kennedy has protested that he is no admirer of the machine, that he deplores its corruptions; and his reputation as a muckraker derives from his antimachine reporting of the early 1960s. But he is also clearly fascinated by its workings. In *O Albany!* and in the novels, fascination seems to overcome disapproval. O'Connell appears as a colorful ole boy, unpretentious, a dictator but a proletarian dictator; Corning is a clever patrician, a survivor with a style. Kennedy seems to enjoy their characters however much he may object to their practices. But he reveals nothing but a cold antipathy toward the third Albany politician to merit a chapter in part 5, the unavoidable Nelson Rockefeller, the governor who stamped Albany with the monumental South Mall complex of marble state government buildings, and in the process razed acres of the Downtown neighborhood. In a similar fashion, Kennedy has expressed his preference for the gangster, Legs Diamond, over the President, Ronald Reagan (Marcus Gorman, the narrator of *Legs,* preferred Legs to Richard Nixon). The morality of these preferences may be dubious, but the sympathies they represent are intelligible. Kennedy's artistic and moral vision focuses upon the vitalities and the vulnerabilities of common people; he has little use for those born to privilege. A Huybertie Pruyn (or, in *Quinn's Book,* a Hillegond Staats) may for particular reasons engage him; a Nelson Rockefeller cannot.

O Albany! constitutes the best introduction to the Albany of William Kennedy. It presents the city in terms of its geography, its history, and its society—its neighborhoods and its politics. It also presents the aspects of the city against which men might indeed rebel; it describes, for example, the exploitative political machine which might well execute a Legs Diamond, ban a Billy Phelan, or pay a Francis Phelan to vote the machine ticket twenty-two times. It is the world Kennedy's heroes must confront.

NOTES

1. Edward C. Reilly, "On an Averill Park Afternoon with William Kennedy," *The South Carolina Review* 21 (1989): 15.

2. William Kennedy, *Ironweed* (New York: Viking, 1983): 169.

3. Michael Robertson, "The Reporter as Novelist," *Columbia Journalism Review* 24 (1986): 52.

4. Robertson 52.

5. William Kennedy, *O Albany!* (New York: Viking, 1983) 5. Subsequent references will be noted in parentheses.

CHAPTER THREE

The Ink Truck

Many of Kennedy's characteristic virtues as a writer are already evident in his first novel, *The Ink Truck* (1969), but they are not, it must be admitted, prevalent. Having read the later Albany novels, one can identify seminal themes and techniques in *The Ink Truck*, but the reader who comes first upon *The Ink Truck* could hardly predict the later Albany novels. The categories of location and dislocation can certainly be applied to *The Ink Truck*, but in this first novel the priority is reversed: the elements of dislocation overwhelm those of location. The concrete, realistic contexts of place, time, and society are largely absent. The novel emphasizes action, and the action focuses upon an explicit rebellion—the strike of a newspaper guild against the newspaper corporation. The narrative proceeds in a self-conscious, discontinuous fashion, employing a variety of surrealistic devices—dreams, extended fantasies, caricatures.

The author's note which Kennedy added to the 1984 reprint of the novel implies that the location of this action is a secondary matter: ''All that needs saying is that this is not a book about an anonymous city, but about Albany,

N.Y., and a few of its dynamics during two centuries."[1] That this does need saying—that the Albany location is not self-evident in every paragraph of the narrative— distinguishes *The Ink Truck* from all of Kennedy's later novels.

The premise of *The Ink Truck*—a strike against a newspaper—was in fact the consequence of a real strike at the Albany *Times-Union;* the unreality of the novel's scene, action, and characters was a deliberate effort to extend its significance. In the actual strike 340 editorial employees, members of Local 34 of the American Newspaper Guild, struck Albany's two Hearst papers, the *Times-Union* and the *Knickerbocker News.* The strike lasted only eighteen days (22 November–10 December 1964), not one year, and the issues were unextraordinary—wages, benefits, work schedules. Some aspects of the strike would be echoed in *The Ink Truck:* there was some violence on the picket line, requiring a court restraining order; the strike, unsupported by the craft unions, did not prevent publication of the papers; and the final award by an arbitrator came closer to management's offer than to the Guild's demands.[2] At the same time that he acknowledged *The Ink Truck's* historical inspiration, Kennedy added, "It was about the civil rights movement, and about being a writer and an individual."[3] These other subjects generalize the meaning of the strike, making it an emblem for rebellion against all establishments, and they mark the hero, Bailey, as more than just a striker. Kennedy has identified Bailey as "an isolated nigger."[4] Bailey is not, of course, black; like all of Kennedy's protagonists, he is Irish, though his Irishness too is less pronounced than that of his successors. But he is an embodiment of oppressed Americans, of those oppressed by a system that prescribes behaviors and punishes deviations. More specifically, he embodies the rebellious energies of those oppressed Americans, and in this sense he may be a 1960s "nigger," asserting his pride and integrity against a dehumanizing system.

And it is of more than biographical significance that the embodiment of that system is a newspaper. The anonymous newspaper company is an industrial concern, with machinery and fences and guards and a public relations department that make it an appropriate symbol of capitalist enterprise. It is also precisely that part of the capitalist establishment dedicated to communicating overtly and covertly the ideology of capitalism. (Neither the novel's hero nor its author advocates Marxism, but these Marxist categories and concepts, an inevitable part of the rhetoric of rebellion in the late 1960s, are certainly relevant to the action and setting of *The Ink Truck*.) Bailey is thus both an alienated proletarian confronting a corrupt and decadent system (and Stanley, the owner of the company, is very corrupt and decadent) and a liberated artist, defying the philistine authority which would dictate the direction of his art.

Bailey is, like his author, a columnist. But where Kennedy devoted himself to the concrete matters of Albany neighborhoods and Albany politics, Bailey's journalism makes no connection with the pedestrian realities of his city. Quite the contrary: he expresses his discontents through a willfully whimsical style. At the beginning of the novel Kennedy establishes the dadaist character of his hero by reprinting a column in which Bailey responds to a reader who has written about his effort "to recapture lost pooka" (19). The reader's letter repeats the nonsense word 23 times (in a 319-word letter); Bailey replies with absurdist aphorisms ("In wartime, an antitank gun will also blow up a corporal").

The reader may be inclined to agree with Bailey's friend Rosenthal: "Bailey's mad" (20). It is Bailey's world, however, that is mad; when the wind is southerly, Bailey knows a hawk from a handsaw. The writer in America in the 1960s—Kennedy or Bailey—puts on an antic disposition because the rotten state of the nation does not lend itself to sober analysis or gradual improvement. A defensive zaniness is Bailey's last resort. It also complicates the interpretation of his experiences.

The strike to which Bailey is committed at the beginning of the novel has at the end of its first year become a farce. The newspaper company, headed by the madman Stanley, has, through guile and mere brutality, reduced the striking Guild from 265 members to 18, and of these, only four remain active: Bailey; the Guild's nominal leader, Jarvis; and Bailey's two friends, Irma and Rosenthal. Jarvis is an officious fool; he will capitulate. Though tempted to retreat, Irma and Rosenthal remain loyal to Bailey and to the ideal of the strike. Bailey, with his energies and his absurdities, *is* the ideal of the strike: he embodies the undefeatable spirit of rebellion against oppressive authority.

Kennedy has called *The Ink Truck* "a willful leap into surrealism."[5] The novel's plot is plausible enough in synopsis. Bailey attempts to sustain the lost cause of the strike. He fails, he suffers, and he abandons his efforts. Then he recovers his commitment and, alone, resumes the strike. Finally, he watches the company seduce all the other characters—fellow workers, relatives, even his wife; only he and Irma and Rosenthal stand in the empty strike headquarters, determined to face the world, at the novel's end. Such a plot might seem to call for social realism in its narration, but the narrative of *The Ink Truck* is not realistic. Instead, it justifies Kennedy's own description of it as "surrealistic." All of the characters except Bailey, Irma, and Rosenthal are to some degree caricatures. Many are genuine grotesques. Bizarre Gypsies and hippies, sexually voracious secretaries and oedipal employers—these are the types which people Bailey's world. Characters are identified only by a single name; they are more the emblems of a disintegrating society than portraits of real people in real circumstances.

The novel's setting is no more realistic than its characters. Despite the author's note, it *is* an anonymous city. No one mentions its name or refers to any definite landmarks. There are hints of Albany. When, in chapter 4, Bailey fantasizes a return to the city of 1832 and discovers pigs running free in the streets, those who have read *O Albany!* or *Quinn's Book* will recognize street pigs as a distinctive feature of Albany life in the early nineteenth century. Passing references to a cholera epidemic and to Dutch authorities in the fantasy chapter, and to the canal (the Erie Canal) and to Cabbageville (= the Cabbagetown described in *O Albany!*) also imply a real location. But these clues are rare and esoteric. The buildings and streets of *The Ink Truck* might be those of any modern city. Kennedy has several times observed that *The Ink Truck* was composed "six inches off the ground";[6] he is speaking of its spirit, but the claim is also true of the novel's topography. The narrative is not grounded in a particular, Albany reality.

And whereas the dates of the action of the later novels will be specified, often to the precise day, the setting of *The Ink Truck* is simply modern. Again there are hints. An allusion to John F. Kennedy near the end of the novel implies a date after 1963, but though the novel does, as Kennedy suggested, reflect the turmoil of the civil rights movement, it does not depict it or any other historical expression of social unrest. There are no identifiable blacks in the novel. The intimations of a counterculture are vague: Skin, the spaced-out advocate of drugs and dropping out, might as easily represent a 1950s beatnik as a 1960s hippie. Deek, the rebel against his upper-middle-class father, does not define his rebellion in any distinctly 1960s terms. Though the theme of the novel is in part political, there are no references to the political traumas, domestic and foreign, which the nation experienced in the 1960s. The politics of *The Ink Truck* are typical, not particular. They represent the struggle between a man and an establishment; neither the man nor the establishment is bound to a historical moment.

The nature of this struggle can best be understood through an examination of the narrative's six-part structure, a structure which roughly follows an epic (or mock-epic) model: the hero appears and engages in battle; he is subjected to trials and temptations; the community for which he fights seems to disintegrate; he visits the underworld and reemerges with a renewed sense of mission; he once again engages in battle; he is once again tempted, but he finally achieves, if not victory, at least integrity. In accord with his surreal intentions Kennedy does not adopt conventional chapter divisions. Each of the six units of the narrative is introduced by a full-page, black-bordered tabloid headline labeled "EXTRA!" A second page offers an epigraph. The headlines do not provide simple titles, but despite their apparent whimsy, they do help to interpret the chapters.

The first headline reads: "A BIZARRE BOLLY FOLLOWS INK CARRIER What Is A Bolly! People Ask" (1). The chapter that follows does not directly answer the people's question, but it does serve to introduce Bailey, who clearly is the Bolly who follows an ink carrier. He follows the carrier in order to sabotage it. He intends to drain the ink truck as a gesture to commemorate the first anniversary of the strike. The gesture miscarries. Though he succeeds in clambering beneath the belly of the truck, Bailey is defeated by the technology of the machinery. But two other, more effective acts of defiance frame the failure and exemplify the extreme violence which accompanies the absurd comedy of Bailey's experience. In the first, Bailey uses a deception to waylay a scab sportswriter who has seduced Guild secrets from Bailey's wife, Grace. Bailey leaves the sportswriter "a bloody-headed figure" on a pile of snow-covered rubble (12). And after his failure beneath the truck, Bailey firebombs the storefront which has been occupied by the Gypsies whom Stanley has brought in as part of his effort to break the strike. Putzina, Queen of the Gypsies, rushes into flames to rescue her life savings and is fatally burned.

Bailey emerges as a man of action. The virtue of his actions may seem debatable, but at least he acts. The Guild's official action marking the anniversary is a silly one-car motorcade directed by Jarvis. Bailey is impetuous and defiant, resilient and humorous. At the end of the chapter, having been beaten by company guards, he responds to Irma's concern for his suffering with the comment, "The trouble with richly endowed women like yourself . . . is that they lack a sense of humor about life" (54). A sense of humor about life is an essential quality of all of Kennedy's heroes. The action of *The Ink Truck* is characterized by wit and whimsy and, at times, even by slapstick humor. The reader is meant to enjoy these. But it is also important that Bailey, as an actor in the action (as victim and as perpetrator), retain his good-humored perspective on the action. A second important quality of Bailey's character is also implied in his comment to Irma. His awareness of her "rich endowments" speaks to his lustiness. An element of bawdry appears in all of Kennedy's books, always as a positive sign of the hero's healthy attitude toward life. *The Ink Truck* is bawdier than most of the novels; Bailey is lustier than most of the heroes. He is a thoroughly (and, some critics might argue, uncritically) virile protagonist—in a word, a Bolly.

The second chapter, "MISSING STRIKER MAY BE VICTIM OF FOUL PLAGUE Black Spots Might Be Sore Points" (55), identifies Bailey with his role as a striker. He is missing because the vengeful Gypsies, led by Putzina's vicious, cynical son, Smith (aka Septimo Ascensor [= Seventh Elevator]) have abducted him from the hospital. The striker is subjected to three exotic experiences, each of which threatens to undermine his sense of himself. Bailey the actor is negated; his arms and legs are bound as he is passed from captor to captor under the distant direction of Stanley. First the Gypsies beat and humiliate him; Bailey replies with crude verbal defiance. Then Skin, formerly an unwashed anarchist who supported the strike, now a glib exponent of hallucinogenic out-of-body experiences, attempts to induce him to drop out; Bailey refuses to be seduced by the prospect of a pseudo-spiritual quest. Finally Miss Blue, Stanley's secretary, invites him to join her in a mechanical parody of sexual bestiality; Bailey declines. Miss Blue has "ORGANIZE ME" painted across her breasts, but, lusty though he is, Bailey will not succumb to the punning temptation. His commitment is to the Guild, however disorganized it may have become.

"GUILD MEMBERS BESET BY WEIRDNESS A Big Mystery It Seems" (107), the title of the third chapter, is the only one without a noun referring to Bailey. In it, the disorganized Guild dissolves, and with its dissolution, Bailey does begin to lose his sense of himself. Popkin, the representative of the International Guild, embarassed by this "all-time champion loser among locals" and especially by the disaster of Bailey's firebombing, dictates an apology which he insists Bailey deliver to Stanley. Bailey's meeting with Stanley provokes the owner into a *Psycho*-like transformation into his own mother. Bailey rebels again, against the gibbering Stanley but also against the pusillanimous Guild. The Guild suspends him. There follows a sequence of disasters: Rosenthal's home is sacked by company thugs; Irma is alienated from her sister; Bailey is alienated from his wife; Smith, the Gypsy, even assassinates the cat upon which Bailey's eccentric Uncle Melvin (once the lover of Putzina) dotes. The chapter ends with Bailey driven "ever deeper into the gloom of guilt" (51).

"PIGS ARE WHERE YOU FIND THEM, OUTLAW DECIDES Soul Is A Pork Chop, He Discovers" (153) presents the first stage of Bailey's recovery of himself. The epigraph of the chapter is drawn from Joseph Campbell's *The Hero with a Thousand Faces,* a passage which argues that faced with death, "there is nothing we can do except be crucified—and resurrected; dismembered totally, and then reborn" (155). In chapters 1 and 2, Bailey was portrayed as the bolly striker; in chapter 3 this identity was dismembered—Bailey was expelled from his membership in the Guild. In this fourth chapter he begins his rebirth through a fantastic dark night of the soul: in a parody of the archetypal action described by Campbell,

Bailey descends into an underworld and acquires the wisdom to resurrect himself as a new figure—the outlaw, beyond the company and the Guild.

He finds his ironic Hades in the underground stacks of the State Library, "one of the city's deepest points." Employed as a shelver, he devotes his time to random readings in the annals of his city. (In this, he may be a figure of Kennedy's own imagination, which discovered its true matter in the annals of Albany.) On the third day he researches the Gypsies and finds a newspaper account of an 1866 incident involving Tercero Ascensor (presumably the great-great-grandfather of Septimo Ascensor, aka Smith). He learns the meaning of the curse which the Gypsies had cast on him following Putzina's death. Oddly enough, the find inspires Bailey to exonerate himself from the crimes of arson and homicide (no civil authority seems ever to judge or even accuse him): "Bailey sensed that if there was a god, then he had certainly incurred divine favor by burning the building and indirectly causing the death of the old woman" (159–60). He concludes that his was "an unpunishable, godlike deed." This self-apotheosis is surely ironic; "indirectly causing the death" is surely a dishonorable evasion.

But if the first result of Bailey's entombment in the State Library is a questionable exculpation, his descent does lead to more fruitful revelations. After a week he renounces his prior illusions, including the illusion of the Guild. In a dialogue with himself he resolves to liberate himself from bondage to the past and the future. Bailey's determination and the absurdist language in which he expresses it again reflect the spirit of the 1960s. It also seems to echo the previously rejected drop-out ethos of Skin, and, emphasizing the echo, Bailey immediately undergoes a sort of out-of-body experience in which he returns to the city of 1832. A cholera epidemic has bred suspicion, internment, and mob violence (all elements of the decade in which Kennedy was writing). Bailey protects a victimized girl and encounters misguided preachers and politicians. In another variation on the chapter's epigraph he observes a seven-year-old child die, return to prate of heaven ("it is a beautiful place," 169) and then to die again. (Another resurrection, dated 1849, opens *Quinn's Book*.) Bailey awakens from his fantasy, like Rip Van Winkle, with a beard and long curved fingernails.

It is not, however, twenty years later. Bailey returns to the upper world in "FAMINE CAN BE FUN BOARD-WALKER TELLS FRIEND And Necessity Turns Out To Be A Mother" (189) and faces the same world. And history seems to repeat itself; he has not escaped his illusions. Bailey undertakes a solitary hunger strike. The other lapsed strikers, including Irma, Rosenthal, and Deek, are reinspired, and begin to picket. Again there is a confrontation with company guards. Again Bailey attempts to drain an ink truck, and this time succeeds in releasing a trickle of ink into the snow.

There are differences. The trickle, however small, is some proof that an individual can make some visible difference. And Bailey now acts autonomously; his rebellious activity lacks even the superficial sanction of the official opposition, the Guild. More important, the quality of the narrative has changed. The Bolly Striker (chapters 1 and 2) encountered a violent but relatively carefree world; the Outlaw Boardwalker (4 and 5) confronts a darker, more hysterical world. The narrative discontinuities of the fourth chapter, with its internal dialogue and its long historical fantasy, continue in the fifth. Bailey has a series of fantasy meetings aboard an ancient trolley. One of these is with Alderman Terence MacSwiney, Lord Mayor of Cork, who advises Bailey: "Try very hard to . . . " (226). In his author's note, Kennedy describes this incomplete phrase as the core of the novel's "political wisdom." Making the effort, not achieving the goal, is a sufficient justification for social struggle.

The hysteria culminates in the final chapter, "ROWDY IS OUSTED AS LAST TROLLEY GOES CLANG, CLANG And the Boon Is On The Spoon" (233). All the major characters (except Skin, who has committed suicide) reunite for a final celebration at Stanley's house. The dinner is drugged, and Stanley presides over a mad orgy in his sauna, performing satanic magic upon his naked guests. Bailey chooses to eat the drugged food, but nonetheless remains apart. When he attempts to fire a pistol, the weapon misfires. Stanley ejects Bailey, Irma, Rosenthal, and—suddenly transformed into another of Stanley's victims—the hitherto evil Smith. The three ex-strikers return to the vacated Guild headquarters, finding it completely bare. "After a long silence they got up and left the room" (278).

And so, despite the penultimate orgy, the novel ends with a whimper. The three protagonists are left at the ellipsis of the Lord Mayor's advice: "Try very hard to . . ." Stanley has vanquished his opposition—the Guild and the entire cast of eccentrics: the painted Miss Blue; Grace, Bailey's roller derby queen wife; the ailurophilic Uncle Melvin; Deek, the would-be proletarian. Mere individualism proves as vulnerable to Stanley's powers and seductions as mere collectivism (the Guild). Only the willful individual, Bailey, and those bound to him by affection and admiration, Irma and Rosenthal, survive. And to what end?

Bailey's final words are a riddle: "I know the sound of one hand clapping, but what is the fruit of the fun tree?" (278). At his orgy Stanley posed as the master of the fun tree, but his play was destructive and dehumanizing. Bailey requires a different answer. In his despair at the midpoint of the novel, Bailey had reviewed the cost of his rebellion: he had suffered at the hands of Smith and the Gypsies, Skin, and Miss Blue; his wife had evicted him from their apartment; the Guild had collapsed. As the third chapter closed, Bailey seemed alienated from all that had given structure to his existence. He reflects: "Solve the riddle or die was the ultimatum he had always lived under. And as he prepared to solve the riddle, he also prepared to die. But he never conceived that the riddle would be taken from him" (151). At this point, then, he was prepared for the absurdities and the fantasies of his descent into the underworld. Now, at the end of his recovery (and the utter dissolution of his dreams), he appropriately produces a new riddle to live for: "What is the fruit of the fun tree?"

In the blank room Bailey had first imagined an aphorism and then a syllogism. These he does not expound. The pseudo-Zen riddle of the fun tree's fruit may seem a sophomoric scripture with which to end a novel, but its purport is clear enough. In a world of violence and exploitation, value lies in continuing to pursue—"very hard," Alderman MacSwiney would add—anything, even the answer to an absurd riddle.

Too ponderous an explication of the morality of *The Ink Truck* would be inappropriate. Much of the pleasure of the novel lies in the mere playfulness of the text. Many aspects of the language and style of the narrative deserve attention. There are, for example, many pigs in *The Ink Truck*. Rising out of the city's history, pigs play a prominent role in the underworld of chapter 4. Chapter 5 (FAMINE CAN BE FUN), by contrast, describes a hunger strike, and it imparts the central wisdom of Alderman Mac*Swiney*. Other animals and animal imagery appear throughout the novel. Uncle Melvin with his cat and Jarvis with his dalmation provide some comic moments. Miss Blue's sexual aberration involves a cow and bull contraption. Bailey nails to his wall composite photos of himself with the heads of a blue pig, a tongueless hound, and a cross-eyed tiger.

In addition to the twenty-page fantasy visit to the city of 1832, there are other dreams and visions which punctuate the narrative. They often emphasize a black and white symbolism: Bailey's vision of black oil trickling down the blade of Smith's knife (39), Irma's dream of frozen blackbirds in a snowy landscape (68), Bailey's dream of Uncle Melvin (137–38). Black and white symbolism is most clearly associated with Bailey's two attempts on the ink truck: the black ink, the white snow. His frustrated attempts to milk the ink truck may be ironically associated with the multitude of breasts he does manage to grasp in a novel whose acronym is, after all, TIT. From his opening grope beneath a neighbor's nightdress, to Irma's full figure, to Miss Blue's painted front, to the proliferation of bosoms at Stanley's orgy, Bailey's world is full of accessible breasts.

Or there is Kennedy's attention to his characters' distinctive costumes—"Bailey and his cossack hat and green muffler; Rosenthal and his cape and Tyrolean feather. This is me, the image said back from the mirror'' (129). Or there are the names dropped throughout the narrative: Aesop, Socrates, Plato, Gibbon, Dumas, Nietzsche, Freud, Joyce, Frost. All of these devices are reminders that *The Ink Truck* is an ambitious first novel. If it must be judged somewhat less successful than Kennedy's remarkable second novel, it must be admitted that it ''tries very hard to . . . ''

NOTES

1. William Kennedy, author's note, *The Ink Truck* (New York: Viking, 1984). Subsequent references will be noted in parentheses.

2. The course of the strike can be traced in *The New York Times* 22 Nov. 1964: 42; 23 Nov. 1964: 30; 29 Nov. 1964: 86; 3 Dec. 1964: 46; 9 Dec. 1964: 61; 10 Dec. 1964: 58; 17 Dec. 1964: 26.

3. Larry McCaffery and Sinda Gregory, ''An Interview with William Kennedy,'' *Alive and Writing* (Urbana: University of Illinois Press, 1987) 171–72.

4. McCaffery and Gregory 168.

5. McCaffery and Gregory 161.

6. McCaffery and Gregory 171; Kay Bonetti, ''An Interview with William Kennedy,'' *The Missouri Review* 8 (1985): 74.

CHAPTER FOUR

Legs

W hen thirty-four-year-old John Thomas Diamond was murdered in his room at 67 Dove Street in Albany (currently the Albany home of William Kennedy) on 18 December 1931, he was one of the most celebrated gangsters in the age of gangsters. He had not been as powerful or successful as Chicago's Al Capone (imprisoned in 1931); Bonny and Clyde and John Dillinger (killed in 1934) would become folk heroes; Dutch Schultz (killed in 1935) had driven Diamond from New York City; Lucky Luciano and Meyer Lansky would supplant Schultz. But Legs Diamond was a notorious figure whose style and good luck led the newspapers to give his activities wide (and often inaccurate) coverage. Although his criminal career began in his native Philadelphia and reached its acme in New York City, he was, at the time of his death, concentrating his forces in the Catskills and preparing to establish himself in Albany. Indeed, Kennedy speculates in *O Albany!* that Diamond's unknown murderers were not the agents of a rival gangster—Dutch Schultz being the most common suspect—but rather the Albany law enforcement establishment which, prompted by Boss O'Connell's political machine, at once eliminated a threat to its own hegemony in the city and county and, as well, warned off future threats. Whoever fired the three bullets into Diamond's head at least assured the gangster's permanent association with Albany, and thus made Legs Diamond an available subject for the imagination of William Kennedy.

But neither his Albany death nor his Irish–American background is sufficient to explain Kennedy's interest in Diamond. The melodrama of his career, of course, provides for an eventful narrative—Diamond commits thefts and murders; he narrowly escapes death, shot on four different occasions prior to 18 December 1831; he faces a series of trials. But even more, he is a gangster. The figure of the gangster has become a familiar icon in twentieth-century American popular culture. W. R. Burnett's *Little Caesar* (1929) and *High Sierra* (1941), Mario Puzo's *The Godfather* (1969), and most recently E. L. Doctorow's *Billy Bathgate* (1989, and featuring Diamond's nemesis, Dutch Schultz) are major works that represent the range of interest in the gangster. Dozens of other novels (as well as many classic and ephemeral films) testify to the fascination of the type. Kennedy's *Legs* (1975) may be the greatest artistic achievement in this genre: its portrait of the gangster's life and times combines historical accuracy with a distinctive perspective and artistic sophistication.

Legs Diamond himself was a special type of gangster. Prior to Prohibition, gangs had been largely local affairs of thugs exploiting neighborhood turfs. Legs Diamond belonged to the transitional generation of charismatic gang leaders whose power extended throughout the city and even beyond its limits. The next generation, embodied in

Charlie "Lucky" Luciano and Meyer Lansky and the evolving American Mafia, would rely more on organization than charisma. It is precisely the charisma of Legs Diamond that Kennedy seeks to examine in *Legs.*

Legs is not a straight, "faction" biography of Jack Diamond, but it does represent a radical shift toward verisimilitude in Kennedy's fiction. The location is not anonymous; Kennedy cites actual addresses in actual cities. The events of the novel correspond to those of the life of the historical Diamond (the endpapers of the hardcover edition present a facsimile "rap sheet" of the criminal career (1916–31) of the actual Jack "Legs" Diamond); the times and places of the novel accurately correspond to the New York scenes of the late 1920s and early 1930s. Kennedy's commitment to mimesis is not, however, absolute. There are, for example, a few surrealist moments: a sailor rolls up his sleeve to show Jack a feathered arm; Jack's mistress, Kiki, has an odd encounter with a penman on the street.[1] And the novel's mystical conclusion demonstrates that a naturalistic presentation of the life and times of Jack Diamond is not Kennedy's entire aim.

Kennedy has given extensive and revealing accounts of the composition of the novel, and these provide some explanation for this abrupt development in his approach to narrative after *The Ink Truck. Legs,* he reports, evolved through eight drafts over a period of six years.[2] His first conception as "a free-floating, ahistorical version" in which Legs Diamond would be viewed was "a mythical generalized gangster."[3] This version seems to reflect something of the dislocated spirit of *The Ink Truck* (Kennedy mentions William Burroughs's *The Last Words of Dutch Schultz* as an analogue). The novelty of this first inspiration was to narrate events from the point of view of a film documentary about Legs Diamond. When this idea generated into a troublesome gimmick—"the cameraman kept getting in the way of the story"[4]—Kennedy abandoned it.

The next approach involved a surrealistic narrative based on the Tibetan Book of the Dead. A vestige of this version survives in the final chapter of *Legs*.[5] Another approach proposed to present the character of Legs entirely through an account of the final day of his life—his acquittal in an important trial, the celebration, the death. The next major development occurred as Kennedy got caught up in researching the actual Jack Diamond. He became "a history junkie" and accumulated stacks of often contradictory contemporary reports.[6] (The "facts" of Diamond's career remain in dispute; even standard reference works provide incompatible details.[7]) Eventually the inconsistencies compelled Kennedy to renounce his "mission" to compose "a meticulously accurate gangster novel."[8] Finally, directly influenced by the prefaces and notes of Henry James and by the example of *The Great Gatsby*,[9] Kennedy arrived at the device of employing the intelligent narrator—Jack's lawyer, Marcus Gorman—plausibly present in the gangster's life, able to embody a personal response to the extraordinary figure, and yet also distant enough to be able to observe and analyze his own responses as well as those of others. Marcus Gorman's account might not be accurate in every detail—much of his information is explicitly hearsay—but his portrait of Jack would be an authentic one.

Gorman serves as an ideal instrument for recording Kennedy's real interest in the novel: not so much to capture the essence of the gangster as to depict the effects of that essence upon others and, ultimately, upon Diamond himself. Kennedy's theme is celebrity, the nature of the magnetic personality. Diamond is a seminal figure in this regard. He acquired—and sought—celebrity at the beginning of the modern age in which the mass media have exhibited the power and the compulsion to create celebrities. Kennedy's Diamond is a gangster, but more importantly he deliberately and flamboyantly *plays* the gangster. Although Kennedy makes a point of having Marcus Gorman note that no one who knows Jack Diamond calls him Legs, the novel is titled *Legs:* the public identity is the crucial one.

Kennedy's interest in this aspect of Legs Diamond is not surprising. Bailey in *The Ink Truck* was also a charismatic figure, a striker who flamboyantly played the striker. Bailey also strongly impressed his associates with his personality; he too was given to dramatic gestures of aggression and violence. And both Bailey and Legs operate nominally through ostracized groups—the Guild and the gang. But neither is really a group man. Diamond's gang is almost as insubstantial as Bailey's disintegrating Guild. Diamond refers to five or six regular gang members and up to twenty-four irregulars, but Kennedy never presents him functioning as a chief executive officer; rather, he depicts a few individual relationships that reflect the interplay between the stylish and forceful leader and his unimaginative underlings.

Unlike Bailey, John Thomas (or John Nolan) Diamond has more than one name—indeed, many more: aka Legs Diamond, John Hart, John Higgins, etc. He is not an archetypal rebel; he is a real, mortal rebel, firmly grounded in time and space. Bailey is an absurd hero who survives in his absurd world as long as he can continue to invent riddles to live by. Legs Diamond is the riddle of *Legs,* a riddle that none of his associates, including his wife, his mistress, and his inquisitive lawyer can solve—a riddle he himself cannot solve. And he does die, killed by three bullets in the head on 18 December 1931. The introduction and conclusion of the novel suggest that in ways he did *not* die, and these must be considered in any interpretation of the text. But Jack Diamond's rebellion is limited by historical contingency and his all too human fate.

The landmarks of Diamond's actual career are presented in the novel: his survival of four attempts on his life (October 1924, October 1927, October 1930, April 1931); his own acts of violence (the Hotsy Totsy Club killing, 1929); the abduction and killing of Harry Western (= Charlie Northrup in *Legs*, 1930); his ill-fated trip to Europe, 1930; the torture of Grover Parks (= Clem Streeter), 1931. The publicized gestures of charity made by the actual Legs—repairing an old woman's cowshed, paying for an ambulance to take a poor woman's son thirty miles to a hospital in Albany—are accurately assigned to the fictional Legs. These events, reported in circumstantial detail by credible reporters, bind the narrative to reality; if there are excesses, they are the excesses of the actual man.

Diamond's women retain their names, but Kennedy has changed the names of most of the minor characters. Diamond's attorney was the prominent Albany lawyer Daniel H. Prior, not Marcus Gorman. The victims of the Hotsy Totsy shooting were Red Cassiday and Simon Walker, not Tim Reagan and Saul Baker. Joe Fogarty, in the novel presented as Diamond's closest lieutenant, presumably substitutes for William Talamo (alias John Scaccio). Harry Western becomes the novel's Charlie Northrup; Grover Parks and James Duncan become Clem Streeter and Dick

Barlett; Jack Storeyhouse becomes Frankie Teller. There are several reasons for these name changes. One is that the names and identities are often confused in the historical record; gangsters, with their many aliases, are not notably honest or forthcoming in such matters. Diamond himself was arrested under several names. More importantly, although the characters and the episodes in which they are involved are identifiable, by changing the names Kennedy reserves the right to alter—to combine, condense, eliminate—nonessential elements in order to produce subordinate characters which are true to type, if not to history.

Some of the minor events of the novel prove to be surprisingly uninvented. Legs Diamond did return to the United States from Bremen on the freighter *Hannover,* and the *Hannover* did carry 4,500 Hartz Mountain canaries in its hold. On the other hand, some of the events are purposeful fabrications. Kennedy creates a brief meeting between Legs and F. Scott Fitzgerald in order to acknowledge an author's debt to *The Great Gatsby* and to invite a comparison between Fitzgerald's gangster protagonists and his own.[10] A third relation between fact and fiction is illustrated in the episode of the German playwright, Weissberg, who naïvely raves over Jack's masterful will to power. It is based on an actual event involving a gangster and a gangster groupie, but the gangster was not Legs and the groupie was not a German playwright.[11] The incident does not alter the plot of Diamond's life, but, based on a gangster reality, it illuminates the theme of the novel.

A final example illustrates a more problematic use of a real but historically unrelated source. One of Diamond's more prominent lieutenants in the novel is the psychopathic Murray (The Goose) Pucinski. The character is, in fact, based on a convicted killer whom Kennedy met in Boston and who claimed to have worked for Diamond. Even if this killer's claim was a self-serving boast, his appearance in the novel can be justified insofar as he represents a type of mentality attracted to the gangster. But The Goose is also given an active role in the plot of *Legs*. Legs orders an unsuccessful attempt to eliminate The Goose and then finds himself hunted by the psychopath. The matter climaxes when The Goose seems to have Legs and Gorman cornered in a bar, and the gangster, the lawyer, and a prostitute named Flossie are compelled to hide in an old peanut butter factory. The episode, which ends with a lovemaking scene between Gorman and Flossie, seems designed more to set up that final connection than to illuminate Legs. The historical Diamond was certainly willing to betray those who worked for him (he abandoned John Scaccio the way Kennedy's Diamond abandoned Joe Fogarty) and was certainly pursued by other gangsters. It is economic to concentrate these aspects of Diamond's life into the Goose episodes, but the invented crisis is perhaps a bit too neatly diverting.

The structure of *Legs* is complex. The novel opens with a brief chapter, "Jack's Alive," set in 1974 as Marcus Gorman convenes a rump session of three people whose lives were touched by Jack—a newsman, a bartender, and a prostitute (Flossie). They meet in one of Jack's old haunts, the bar of the Kenmore Hotel, and they testify to their undiminished awe of the gangster's powerful personality. The chapter ends with Gorman recalling the summer day in 1930 when Diamond summoned him from Albany and offered to employ him. The body of the novel, the next seven chapters, moves forward from Gorman's first incidental encounters with Jack in 1925 and 1929 ("Jack

Sauce''), through his year and a half of service to the gangster, to an account of Diamond's final day of life, 18 December 1931 ("Jack O' the Clock"). In between, Gorman covers the major events he was involved in: the summer 1930 summons ("Jack, Out of Doors"); Jack's unsuccessful foray to Europe in September 1930 ("Johnny Raw, Jack Gentleman''); Jack's third escape from assassination in October 1930 ("Playing the Jack"); Jack's fourth escape in April 1931, and the extended drama of his kidnapping and torture of Clem Streeter and the sequence of trials in summer and fall 1931 ("John Thomson's Man," "Jack among the Maids," and "Jack-in-the-Box"). "Jack O' the Clock" finally returns the narrative to the Kenmore bar in 1974, with the four survivors convinced that Jack is still somehow alive, a vital force in their lives. In the novel's short epilogue, "Jacked Up," the narrative returns to December 1931, to the "incipiently dead" Jack Diamond, and describes the moment from Jack's point of view. Nearly all of the action is recollected: Gorman recalls his own experiences with Jack and reports the remainder of Jack's activities through the recollections of others—Jack's men, Jack's women, Jack himself. As a result, although the body of the narrative moves steadily forward from summer 1930 to December 1931, it also leaps backward to memories of the past and forward to, for example, the fates of Kiki and Alice after Jack's death.

Very few of the episodes of the narrative are presented in a simple past tense. Even those in which Gorman himself was a participant—the day in the Catskills, the voyage to Europe—are qualified by his awareness of the discrepancy between the young Gorman who gave up thoughts of a political career in order to attach himself to a flamboyant gangster and the old Gorman who gathers with cronies to relive that shared attachment. This awareness is inherent in the narrative. As he goes to meet Jack for the first time, for example, Gorman reports:

> We got into Jack's custom, two-tone (green and gray) Cadillac sedan with whitewalls and bulletproof glass, armor panels, and the hidden pistol and rifle racks. The latter were features I didn't know existed until the following year when Jack had the occasion to open the pistol rack one fateful night (32).

The narrator must draw upon three time frames to compose this passage. The first is that of the moment itself, the summer Sunday in 1930 when the nervous young Gorman noticed the superficial details of Jack Diamond's car—the green and gray, the whitewalls. The second is that of April 1931, when Kiki watched Jack use the concealed pistol to stop and abduct the bootlegger Clem Streeter, the "fateful" crime which led to Jack's most important trial. The third is the indefinite date "the following year" (1931, sometime after April) when Kiki recounted her memory of the abduction to Gorman and Gorman added one more piece to his mosaic of the amazing Jack. One function of this particular example is to create suspense—the "fateful night" when Jack reveals the sedan's secrets occurs 165 pages after Gorman's innocent first ride. But it illustrates the general complexity of the retrospective narration.

And most of the episodes are doubly retrospective as Gorman recalls the recollections of others. Jack, Flossie, Kiki, Alice, Fogarty, The Goose all share their memories of Jack's life. Clem Streeter tells his version of his abduction (overheard by Gorman in 1933 while sitting in a bar-bershop). Minor characters like Jesse Franklin, Jack's black cook, and Sal, a waiter at the Kenmore, contribute their particular perspectives in their own voices. Jesse: "But I say to myself, Jesse, you ought to know what's goin' on hereabouts. . . . So I takes my flashlight and I spokes quietlike down them stairs" (134). Sal: "You ask me was he an animal, a beast—I say no. He was a fanat. . . . He must've had some kind of good in him, I gotta say it. Not for the moneywise he gave me" (238).

This variety of perspectives enables Kennedy to pursue his principal theme: the nature of celebrity. Each narrator adds a fragment to Jack's history and at the same time reveals how that fragment impressed him or her. Jesse's troubled discovery of the remains of Jack's violence (the dismembered body of a rival) and Sal's naïve awe of Jack's sexual daring (openly living with Alice and Kiki at the same time) represent credible contemporary responses to Jack's way of living. Jesse is horrified, and leaves Jack ("These is bad people," he tells Marcus); he winds up in an Albany flophouse. Sal, who arrives at no insight— "But, actually speaking, who's a know what the hell really goes on upstays?" (238)—has the useful thrill of having been near a celebrity; he has a great story to tell his friends.

Everyone expresses some reaction to Legs. Jesse is exceptional in the unequivocality of his moral disapproval, and even he had been in awe of his employer. A Minneapolis librarian whom Jack seduces on the voyage to Europe concludes, "You turn women into swine" (85). The two women who dominate his life in Kennedy's account have more complex reactions. Although Alice and Kiki are not simply Mother and Whore, their struggle for sexual hegemony is, in part, a struggle between the appeals of an attractive wife and an exciting mistress. Neither is able to command Jack's exclusive attentions; both need the stimulation of his presence. Both respond to his completeness as a man, but for Kiki, Jack is a source of intense pleasure ("fucking is one thing and fucking with Jack was another thing altogether" [150]); for Alice, Jack is a virile husband who needs to be recalled to the duties of marriage and the church. Their different responses to Jack are epitomized in the ways they seek to capitalize on his death. Both travel the burlesque and vaudeville circuit, Kiki as a dancer ("the Gangster's Gal"); Alice as the heroine of a moralistic skit ("The straight and narrow is the only way" [302]). These alternative views of Jack are, to a degree, parallel to those of Sal and Jesse. Mere excitement or disapproving excitement seem to be the common reactions to Legs Diamond.

But the two most important responses to the phenomenon of Legs are those of the narrator, Marcus Gorman, and of the hero himself, John Thomas Diamond. Gorman spends a year and a half in the company of a man who "was alive in a way that I was not" (36), who had a "luminous quality" (105). He toasts Diamond in Albany after his acquittal, "Jack, we need only your presence to light us up like Times Square in fervid and electric animation. You are the undercurrent of our lives. You turn on our light . . . " (289). This excessive yet evidently sincere rhetoric coming from a worldly lawyer is a testimony to the gangster's charisma.

Gorman is not merely a Nick Carraway, passively fascinated by the vitality of an extraordinary man. He is altered by the experience. On that first summer's day Diamond presses Gorman to play with his new toy, a Thompson submachine gun. Gorman calls the thrill he receives from firing the weapon at a poster of Dutch Schultz "my little moral collapse" (41); larger collapses follow. By September he has abandoned his ambition of running for Congress; he has smuggled money for Jack; and he has committed what he calls a "quasi-rape." But he observes, "My life had changed in startling ways I wouldn't yet say I regretted" (122). In the end Marcus will justify Jack's torture of Clem Streeter—"A few burns to the feet and ankles are picayune compared to what might have happened" (230)—and will unscrupulously labor to exonerate the torturer in court (at the same time, he abandons Jack's impoverished and unstylish accomplice, Fogarty, to his fate). In a key passage Gorman remarks that he, his pious father, and Jack have in common an Irish Catholic "religious confusion"; his father and Jack "have misplaced tomorrow and are looking for it. And the search is ruining today" (257–58). Gorman can envy the intensity of Jack's life, recognize its violence and its sensuality, and at the same time regard the violent sensualist as a spiritual father figure.

Toward the end of the novel, in an incident based on fact, Jack says in an interview with the *Daily News,* "This stuff written about me has created a mythical figure in the public mind. Now I'm Jack Diamond and I've got to defend myself against the mythical crimes of the mythical Legs" (243). His protest is disingenuous and self-serving, but there is a sense in which the cultivated legend of Legs Diamond does become an external force influencing the life of Jack Diamond. Kennedy has observed, "Diamond fascinated the public the way a movie star does."[12] The 1920s and 30s saw the apotheosis of both movie stars and gangsters. Gorman notes that when *Public Enemy* (1931) played in Albany, Jimmy Cagney was advertised as a imitation of Legs. And, reciprocating the compliment, Legs borrows from Hollywood: Jack "read every newspaper story and book and saw every movie about gangland. . . . It was one way of keeping tabs on his profession" (74). Jack is the master of the dramatic gesture: repairing a widow's cowshed; flinging a fortune of jewels into the sea; firing a pistol between the legs of a fatuous playwright; telling a kid, "Stay in school. The rackets are a bum life" (258). This last good deed was echoed by Cagney at the end of *Public Enemy*.

Marcus Gorman realizes the power of the media's image of Legs as early as the voyage to Europe: "The press of the whole Western world was following our transatlantic voyage," and he observes that the reporters, "installing Jack in the same hierarchy where they placed royalty, heroes, and movie stars, created him anew as they enshrined him" (89). By inventing interviews and embellishing facts, the newsmen expropriate Jack. "This voyage had the effect of taking Jack Diamond away from himself, of making him a product of the collective imagination. Jack had imagined fame all his life and now it was imagining him" (89). This is a central statement of the theme of *Legs*. Kennedy's original notion, that of adopting the cameraman's view of Legs, would have made the same point. A celebrity is not simply located in time and space; he is also located in—defined and limited by—his place in the popular imagination, a place determined by the words and images of the mass media. The two locations are not identical: Jack Diamond is the existential gangster; Legs is the essential Gangster.

The humorous encounter between Jack and the German playwright, Weissberg, reveals the difference. Weissberg responds to the Gangster with Nietzschean rhapsodies.

Accompanied by his "dirty little whore" he meets Jack in a restaurant garden in Bremen and proclaims the identity of "the great artist, the great whore, and the great criminal":

> And I see the great criminal shining through the bold perversion of his deeds, in his willingness to scale the highest moral barriers (and what is morality to the whore, the artist?) . . . We live, you and I, Herr Diamond, in the higher realms of the superman. We have each overcome our troublesome self. We exist in a world of will (109–10).

Jack does exist in a world of will; but he does not intellectualize his existence; he does not believe in "Legs." His response to Weissberg's rhetoric is to walk over to a bodyguard and return with a small pistol which he fires into the grass between Weissberg's legs. He then pays for the drinks and departs, leaving the playwright with wet pants and a tearful face. Weissberg sees "Legs"; Jack sees through Weissberg.

The character of "Legs" is also revealed in the mail Jack receives as he recuperates from his 1930 shooting: writers want him to drown their kittens, protect them as they cheat their bookies, kill their ungrateful sons. He has become the notorious epitome of toughness. The degree to which he has been absorbed by the popular imagination is reflected in the proposal of the impresario Lew Edwards, that Legs turn to old-time religion and undertake a profitable evangelical revival tour—"a million dollar idea" (185). Jack rejects the notion; he retains—up to the epilogue, at least—a sense of the reality of his situation.

Jack's heroism, to Marcus Gorman, lies in his ability to maintain a balanced view of his two locations, in reality and in myth. He is neither limited by a pedestrian view of his possibilities nor seduced by grandiose visions of his own significance. Both elements are present in Gorman's first day with Jack, as he encounters the brutal realities of gangland power—submachine guns and crushed canaries—but also follows Jack through the underbrush to hear him imagine the building of a grand house with a panoramic view of the Catskills. Jack's masterful handling of Alice and Kiki throughout the narrative is a constant symbol of his balance. The word itself is used by Gorman to describe Jack at crucial moments. At the time Jack rejects Lew Edwards's million-dollar idea, Gorman notes that the gangster "was in the midst of a delicate, supremely honest balancing act that would bring his life together if it worked" (191). Gorman sees Jack's task while he awaits his final trial as "the balancing of the forces of his life in a way that would give him ease" (235). Balance, however, does not imply moderation. Jack merely wanted different extremes at the same time—Kiki *and* Alice. One of his most impressive moments occurs at the end of his life as he escorts Kiki and Alice to the Rain-Bo Room of the Kenmore Hotel. Gorman watches to see which woman gets the first dance. Jack elegantly solves the dilemma by waltzing with both of them at once. This acme of balance is placed at the end of the chapter "Jack among the Maids." The next chapter, "Jack-in-the-Box," begins the account of his trials.

Diamond influences people, those who know him as Jack and those who read him as Legs. He also influences the lives of people like Wilson, the high roller who challenged Arnold Rothstein; and Billy Blue, the gunman who attempted to kill him; and his old pal Charlie Northrup; and the "nigger" who drew a knife when Jack was hijacking his truck; and Tim Reagan; and Red Moran; and Tony (The Boy) Anapola—Jack is the terminal influence on these lives. He is a killer. Kennedy takes the novel's epigraph from Ionesco: "People like killers. And if one feels sympathy for the victims it's by way of thanking them for letting themselves be killed." There is very little sympathy for the victims in *Legs*. They are all themselves criminals; and they lack Jack's style, Jack's balance, Jack's luck.

But people did like and admire Jack. Robert Warshow's analysis of the emergence of the gangster as an American folk hero in the 1930s—"The Gangster as Tragic Hero"—may be relevant here. Warshow argues that the gangster is a simplified and extreme example of the American drive for success. He embodies in a pure brutal form the aggressive energies which, more or less sublimated, are the key to advancement in ordinary business. "The gangster's whole life is an effort to assert himself as an individual, to draw himself out of the crowd, and he always dies *because* he is an individual; the final bullet thrusts him back, makes him, after all, a failure."[13]

Jack *is* a businessman, though the narrative emphasizes the remarkable consequences of his industry rather than the mundane methods through which he acquires his wealth. Marcus actually inventories his stock at one point: $3.8 million of rye whiskey, $2 million of champagne, etc. (232). He competes for sources and outlets; he makes deals and borrows capital; he plans a fine house in the country; he pursues Benjamin Franklin's injunction to look after appearances. But he controls his market through the direct assertion of his physical power and presence; he risks death, not bankruptcy. His is the extreme pursuit of success at the junction of the Roaring Twenties and the

Depression Thirties. Warshow observes, "At bottom, the gangster is doomed because he is under the obligation to succeed, not because the means he employs are unlawful. In the deeper layers of the modern consciousness, *all* means are unlawful, every attempt to succeed is an act of aggression, leaving one alone and guilty and defenseless among enemies: one is *punished* for success."[14] This may be why Legs so fascinated his contemporaries, from Sal the waiter to Marcus Gorman to the mother who wanted him to kill her ungrateful son. Jack's appeal lies in his willingness to balance extreme forces. Everyone else makes compromises; they risk a bit of aggression, but never too much. Jack wants all and risks all. And everyone knows that because of his uncompromising pursuit of power and pleasure, Jack is doomed—including Jack, who confesses to Kiki that he doesn't expect to live to be thirty-three.

This is a principal source of Jack's appeal to William Kennedy. In a discussion of *Legs* he acknowledges that all his books deal with "the treatment of characters in extreme conditions."[15] All see themselves as somehow disenfranchised by their societies; all respond by becoming outlaws of some sort. Jack in the unadulterated outlaw. And he is distinguished from the others by his unembarrassed exercise of raw power. In an unequal struggle, others assert their integrities against corrupt political, social, and economic systems—Bailey versus the newspaper and the Guild. Jack, with his gang and his fame and a good lawyer, is almost the equal of the establishment against which he opposes himself. He does draw himself out from the crowd. He does achieve, briefly, success. And though, as Warshow's analysis prescribes, a final bullet (actually three bullets) thrusts him back, his individuality survives his death. When the 1974 frame story resumes at the end of the novel, Marcus Gorman and his friends express the sense of Jack's lasting power by telling tales—how Jack could snap his fingers and turn on lights, run up walls and across ceilings, outrun rabbits, tie both his shoes at once. Forty-three years after his death Jack remains alive. In the novel's first words Gorman had begun the frame (and the project of re-creation through recollection) by announcing, "I really don't think he's dead."

Jack doesn't think so either. Gorman speaks the novel's first line; at the close of the peculiar epilogue, dead Jack Diamond speaks its last: "I really don't think I'm dead." The epilogue, with its strange account of Jack's spirit *not* dissolving upward into "brilliant whiteness," but instead falling backward, destined, Kennedy has said in an interview, "to be reborn, maybe in the gutters of Calcutta, or somewhere other than in that whiteness, perpetuated in this society by people like Marcus, and me, who have retold the legends that grew up around him,"[16] is a survival of the version of the novel based on the Tibetan Book of the Dead. Whatever its mystical implications, it is appropriate that the final view of Jack be Jack's, and that it emphasize his spirit's inability to separate itself from Leg's immortal identity as a legendary gangster. As long as Marcus can gather with old friends in the Kenmore Hotel (or as long as people read *Legs*), Jack Diamond isn't dead.

Although Kennedy composed a screenplay of *Legs* in 1983 ("with a more linear presentation" than the book[17]) with the hope of seeing it filmed by Francis Ford Coppola, people cannot yet *watch* Legs Diamond. (Kennedy did complete a third version of the screenplay in 1989). But, ironically, they can watch Kennedy's version of Diamond's archadversary, Dutch Schultz. Kennedy's contributions to the Coppola film *The Cotton Club* are difficult to assess because of the peculiar collaboration. Mario Puzo composed four scripts, all of which were put aside. Coppola then wrote two scripts. Kennedy was then commissioned to assist in revising the plot and dialogue. He himself describes the final version as the product of an "ensemble."[18] Kennedy's view of Dutch Schultz as a contrasting type of the gangster is perhaps most interesting: "Schultz was nowhere near as appealing a character as Diamond was to me. And that's the way we played him."[19] In a distinction he has drawn several times, Kennedy compares Schultz with Al Capone: they are the brutes, the pigs. Diamond is the cobra. Schultz is the slob with gravy on his tie; Diamond is the sharp dresser with the flashy style. Schultz is the ruthless businessman; Diamond is the "cowboy."[20] The contrasts emphasize Diamond's appeal as an rebel who opposes his personal style against brutal organizations—the businessmen of the upper or underworlds.

NOTES

1. William Kennedy, *Legs* (New York: Coward, McCann, 1975) 113, 155–6. Subsequent references will be noted in parentheses.

2. Kay Bonetti, "An Interview with William Kennedy," *The Missouri Review* 8 (1985): 72.

3. Larry McCaffery and Sinda Gregory, "An Interview with William Kennedy," *Alive and Writing* (Urbana: University of Illinois Press, 1987) 164.

4. Bonetti 72.

5. Bonetti 80; McCaffery and Gregory 162.

6. McCaffery and Gregory 165.

7. The "facts" of Diamond's life presented in this chapter derive from three such sources: Craig Thompson and Allen Raymond, *Gang Rule in New York* (New York: Dial, 1940); Jay Robert Nash, *Bloodletters*

and Badmen (New York: M. Evans, 1973); and Carl Sifakis, *The Encyclopedia of American Crime* (New York: Facts on File, 1982).

8. McCaffery and Gregory 165.

9. Bonetti 72; McCaffery and Gregory 166–67.

10. Bonetti 84; McCaffery and Gregory 166–67.

11. David Thomson, "The Man Has Legs," *Film Comment* 21 (1985): 58.

12. Bonetti 73.

13. Robert Warshow, "The Gangster as Tragic Hero," *The Immediate Experience* (New York: Atheneum, 1974) 133.

14. Warshow 133.

15. Bonetti 73.

16. McCaffery 162.

17. Thomson 58.

18. Edward C. Reilly, "On an Averill Park Afternoon with William Kennedy," *The South Carolina Review* 21 (1989): 17; Thomson 55.

19. Reilly 18.

20. Reilly 18; Thomson 58.

CHAPTER FIVE

Billy Phelan's Greatest Game

In *Legs*, William Kennedy began to exploit the essential matter of his fiction: the concrete realities of Albany. But Jack Diamond turns to Albany only at the end of his life, and then only of necessity. Marcus Gorman is a native and, like Diamond, an Irish–American; and he is the only character in *Legs* to reappear in Kennedy's later novels. But though his Albanian perspective is thematically central in *Legs*, he is himself clearly secondary to the charismatic gangster. In his later novels Kennedy focuses the action entirely upon native Albanians. *Billy Phelan's Greatest Game* (1978) establishes this new orientation.

In fact, *Billy Phelan's Greatest Game* derives from Kennedy's very first attempt at long fiction—the unpublished novel, *The Angels and the Sparrows*. Kennedy began work on this narrative in Puerto Rico. It ranges through sixty years in the lives of the Irish–American Phelan family of Albany. The original of Francis Phelan first appeared there. When Kennedy began to write *Billy Phelan's Greatest Game*, he decided to make Billy the son of Francis (and so was compelled to create Annie as Francis's wife and Billy's mother).[1] Though similarly altered and amplified, the characters and events of his last three novels have drawn upon this common source. George Quinn, minor character in *Billy Phelan's Greatest Game,* is the grandson of the Daniel Quinn of *Quinn's Book* (1988). George Quinn's wife is Billy's sister, Margaret (Peg); their son is ten-year-old Daniel Quinn, the protagonist of the short stories "The Secrets of Creative Love" (1983) and "An Exchange of Gifts," (1985–86). Peg and young Daniel appear in an important scene in *Ironweed* (1983).

Billy Phelan's Greatest Game covers a crucial week in the life of Billy Phelan, like William Kennedy, a scion of a Catholic working-class family, Irish on all sides. The action begins on Thursday, 20 October 1938, and Billy is a carefree thirty-one-year-old, living off his skill and his luck at games—bowling, poker, pool—and off the profits of his small bookmaking operation. In the course of a few days he learns that his way of life is contingent not just upon his skill and luck, but also upon the whim of the political powers which control the locations in which the games are played. Unlike Bailey and Jack Diamond, Billy Phelan does not choose to rebel against his society; rather, his society seems to move against him. His reluctant decision not to compromise his integrity, not to accept the new rules imposed by the powers, forces him into isolated resistance.

The character of the political reality of Billy Phelan's world—the reality of the unlimited power of Boss O'Connell's Democratic machine—was an essential part of Kennedy's conception. The kidnapping of O'Connell's nephew, which provides a central plot of the novel, actually took place in 1933; the machine's successful subversion of the American Labor Party (headed by Jake

Berman in the novel) did not take place until the 1940s. But Kennedy wanted to set his drama of conflict between the individual and the machine in an election year.[2] In 1938 Thomas E. Dewey, the Republican, antimachine candidate for a governor, lost a close election to Herbert Lehman. The machine's power is illustrated in the novel when it shuts down all electricity in the county during one of Dewey's campaign speeches. (Dewey would win the next election, in 1942, but *O Albany!* chronicles the impotence of his reforms.) Dewey's one significant achievement in eliminating the machine's election fraud in the 1938 election appears to be the arrest of a man—Francis Phelan—for voting the machine ticket twenty-one times. Billy Phelan's Albany was, Kennedy has said, "a controlled environment" in which "everyone kowtowed, everyone had fear, because Dan O'Connell (or Patsy McCall in *Billy Phelan*) owned the city," and in which "the individual became a totally subordinate figure whose freedom was very much in question."[3] A major theme of the novel emerges through Billy's belated discovery of the potential for conflict between his own moral code and the demands made upon him by the machine.

Kennedy introduces a new motif in his portrayal of Billy's social dislocation. In addition to the problem of defining his position relative to the political realities of Albany, Billy also faces the special problem of clarifying his relationship to his father. Bailey and Jack Diamond (and Marcus Gorman) were parentless; fathers (and father figures) and sons become primary pairs in the later novels. (Kennedy dedicates *Billy Phelan's Greatest Game* to his own son, Brenden.) To reinforce the theme in the novel, Kennedy introduces Martin Daugherty as a second protagonist. Daugherty, from whose point of view much

Billy Phelan's Greatest Game

of the novel is narrated, is an older man who advises and supports Billy. He is also engaged in his own struggle to come to terms with his own father and his own son. In addition to locating themselves in Albany, Kennedy's protagonists now have the task of locating themselves in the generations of their families.

The novel opens with Billy playing one of his greatest games—bowling 299 in an alley of the Downtown Health and Amusement Club and beating Scotty Streck. The scene is exactly the sort that captures Kennedy's imagination. He described their draw upon him in *O Albany!* and he has written a personal memoir about these same bowling alleys—and about the bowling accomplishments of his uncle, Pete McDonald, the prototype of Billy Phelan ("My Life in the Fast Lane"). His description of the game in the first chapter of *Billy Phelan's Greatest Game* illustrates his ability to re-create in fiction these significant artifacts of Albany past.

But the competition is not merely a period set piece. Kennedy uses the occasion to introduce the characters and the forces which motivate the action of the novel. Billy Phelan, seen through Martin Daugherty's sympathetic eyes, is the central figure. Martin, a journalist, views Billy as a "low-level maestro" of all games. He played baseball in a city league, he can deal cards, shoot pool, throw dice, toss darts. He is a champion drinker and a small-time bookie. And for reasons which he cannot specify, Martin finds himself fascinated by the younger man. He has known Billy since his birth, and had known Billy's father, Francis, until Francis mysteriously abandoned his family when Billy was nine.

Morrie Berman, who backs Billy with a $200 wager, is a gambler and ex-pimp, the son of a politically radical

Jew—another important father-son relationship. Berman's violent reaction to Scotty Streck's poor sportsmanship—hexing Billy's shot at a perfect game—contrasts with Billy's cool acceptance. Billy's later refusal to inform on Morrie will lead to his troubles in Albany. Charlie Boy McCall, who backs Scotty Streck, is another central character. Charlie Boy is the son of Bindy McCall and the nephew of Patsy McCall. The McCalls are Kennedy's version of the actual O'Connell family which ran Albany from the 1920s to the 1970s. Patsy McCall represents Boss Dan O'Connell, the man who controlled the Democratic machine which controlled Albany. Boss Dan assigned responsibility for the lucrative regulation of Albany's nightlife—the speakeasies, the gambling—to his brother, John (Solly). Patsy McCall assigns the identical responsibility to his brother, Benjamin (Bindy). It is Bindy McCall who set Billy up as a card dealer in Saratoga; it is Bindy who sanctions Billy's bookmaking and who oversees Billy's regular payments for the sanction. Bindy's son, Charlie, is the only male McCall of his generation, and his kidnapping provokes the crisis of the novel.

Martin Daugherty keeps score during the bowling game; in a sense he keeps score throughout the novel. In this first chapter, Martin, aged fifty, observes that Billy, at thirty-one, "seemed fully defined."[4] By contrast, when he himself had been thirty-one, his own father had called him a failure. And he wishes his own son, Peter, aged fourteen, had some of Billy's "scarred sassiness" (8). He recalls the time when he acted as a surrogate father to fourteen-year-old Billy when Billy had smashed a finger with a bowling ball. These interlocking symmetries immediately identify Martin with the theme of the continuities and discontinuities of fathers and sons.

They also establish Martin's character in contrast to Billy's. The action of the novel is presented through the alternating perspectives of Billy and Martin. Billy seems to exist in the moment, focusing his energies on the game at hand, relying on his "sassiness" to carry him through. He shows little foresight, the most obvious example being his crucial failure as a small-time bookie to lay off part of Martin Daugherty's wager, and he seems to take little account of the past. He is not consciously searching for his father. He is naïvely surprised when his girlfriend presents him with the prospect of fatherhood. Martin, by contrast, is all too aware of his place in time. Even as he watches Billy bowl, he dwells upon the future of his own errant son. With his reflections on his own and Billy's pasts and his perpetual thoughts about his father and his son, Martin represents an intelligence preoccupied with time past and time future. That he proves to be endowed with a peculiar form of precognition emphasizes this orientation. The action of the novel is filtered through these two minds, one reactive, the other meditative.

The main plot of the novel begins in chapter 2 on the day after the bowling match. Martin learns that Charlie Boy has been abducted. He forces himself into the counsels of the McCalls and learns that they already suspect Morrie Berman. The kidnappers ask for a quarter-million-dollar ransom, and the McCalls publish a list of acceptable go-betweens, including Morrie and Billy. Billy is summoned to the McCalls and asked to watch Berman; when he and Martin notice that Morrie lies about a hoodlum being in Newark, Billy informs Bindy, but adds that he will not cooperate further. Bindy responds by ostracizing Billy. Morrie is selected as the go-between and with Martin he delivers a $40,000 ransom in New York City.

Charlie Boy is released. Two kidnappers, Maloy and Curry, are seized in Newark, though this proves to be a coincidence. Morrie is arrested; his father arranges to have Legs Diamond's lawyer, Marcus Gorman, defend him. Martin Daugherty writes a column which shames the McCalls into withdrawing the ban they placed on Billy.

Kennedy recounts the historical basis for this plot in *O Albany!* In 1933 (not 1938) John (Solly) O'Connell's son, John Jr. was kidnapped and held for twenty-three (not four) days. The ransom demand was the same ($250,000); the ransom collected was the same ($40,000). John Jr. was also released unharmed. Eight men were eventually arrested; four were from Albany. One was Manny Strewel, the man who served as the go-between. Strewel was defended by Legs Diamond's lawyer, Daniel H. Prior. Kennedy does not report what success Gorman had in defending Berman; Manny Strewel was convicted and sentenced to fifty years. The conviction was overturned on appeal, and before a second trial could be held, Strewel pleaded guilty to a lesser charge, blackmail, and was sentenced to fifteen years. Later a federal court also convicted him of extortion. He served his time, and was reported alive in 1983.

There was no Billy Phelan involved in the O'Connell kidnapping, but then there was no Billy Phelan involved in the McCall kidnapping either. Billy is not an accomplice, and does not even knowingly possess relevant information. But his refusal to spy on Morrie Berman leads to the crisis in which he is compelled to recognize the limited extent to which he controls his fate in Albany. The machine's power had been a familiar reality, and he had casually benefited from its benevolence. In the midst of the Great Depression the machine provided sources of income, more or less legitimate, for those who came from the right neighborhoods and contributed to the right campaigns. But when Bindy McCall tells Billy, "All, right, hotshot, you're all by yourself" (198), he does not merely cut off Billy's source of income; he effectively cancels Billy's identity as a man in Albany.

The kidnapping plot, distributed in half a dozen of the novel's twenty chapters, forms the skeleton of the narrative; its flesh is Kennedy's depiction of the demimonde of Albany in 1938—the world in which Billy and Martin take their pleasures and live their lives. Billy is presented as the quintessential player, a person who takes risks. "Men like Billy Phelan," Martin observes, "forged in the brass of Broadway, send, in the time of their splendor, telegraphic statements of mission: I, you bums, am a winner" (8). Billy *is* a winner. In addition to his near perfect bowling game, he spots a sucker forty points in a pool game and wins. He wins an important poker hand on what may have been a bluff, and he spots a cheater and skillfully eliminates him from the game. Finally he boldly disarms a young pistol-waving bandit who interrupts the game. (Earlier he had as boldly disarmed a knife-wielding madman in a luncheonette.) In games and in matters of life and death Billy takes chances; and with what Martin called "sassiness," he wins.

Billy loses twice in *Billy Phelan's Greatest Game,* and both occasions are significant. In one, he is beaten by a pool hustler, Doc Fay. Later Billy reveals to Martin that he lost deliberately in an unsuccessful effort to relieve himself of his obligations to Morrie Berman. The logic of the affair is convoluted, but the episode illustrates the seriousness with which Billy holds to his personal code of honor. At another point he readily accepts the services of a $1.50 prostitute, but he reacts violently to attack her pimp when he boasts of having had intercourse with his own sister.

Billy's other loss occurs when Martin, playing a hunch after learning of Charlie Boy's abduction, uses Billy as his bookie for a three-horse parlay in which he bets on three long shots with "Charlie" in their names. The parlay pays off, and because he had laid off none of the $40 wager, Billy himself must come up with Martin's $788. Again, his code requires him to pay the debt in full, and this determination drives him to the pool match and the poker game: he will repay his gambling obligation by gambling. The world of games is his only world, and all the citizens of that world—bowlers, pool hustlers, card sharks—recognize him. Martin summarizes his character: "a strong man, indifferent to luck, a gamester who accepted the rules and played by them, but who also played above them, . . . a serious fellow who put play in its proper place: an adjunct to breathing and eating" (200).

Bindy McCall's orders isolate Billy from this world which recognizes him. The bartender at his regular bar, Becker's, allows him, as a special favor, one last drink. "Not wanted in Becker's? That's like a ball game with no home plate" (238). Billy's instinctive simile could be extended: he discovers that his Albany has become a closed ball park. No bar wants his money; no game wants his play. Earlier in the novel Billy happened to recall a parallel case. A pathetic robber named Georgie Fox had been marked lousy by Bindy and had found Albany closed to him: "the gin mills, the card games, the gambling joints, the pool rooms, the restaurants, the night clubs, even the two-bit whorehouses" (87). Billy had given him occasional hand-outs. But after two years of being ostracized,

Billy Phelan's Greatest Game

Georgie had climbed a viaduct and leapt seventy feet to his death. "Why didn't they just beat on him a little," Billy wondered. Lock him up or take away what he owned? But they took away the whole world he lived in" (88).

Now they—the McCalls—have taken away Billy's whole world. He is reduced to the companionship of Slopie Dodds, a black derelict. Alone, Billy spends a cold night beside the Hudson River. He considers suicide, but resists. In an explicit imitation of his father's flight from Albany twenty-two years previously, he resolves to flee, to "pack his bag and hop a freight" (258). He pukes, and he heads home. This night, the nadir of his young life, alters Billy radically. As he walks home, "Billy knew he'd lost something he didn't quite understand, but the onset of the mystery thrilled him" (259). He lacks the maturity to realize fully what has happened to him—his father, Francis, will possess the maturity in *Ironweed*—but he is aware in a new way of his place in the world. In the novel's final chapter, after Martin Daugherty's newspaper column has restored him to the world of Albany games and bars, Billy reflects on his night by the river. Had he committed suicide, he would have been a "sucker," that most despised category of player. Instead, he discovered in himself the strength to endure dislocation. He knows that he has been permanently marked as a "renegade"; there will always be a residual alienation between him and the Albany of the McCalls. In his column, Daugherty had written that Billy was "touched with magic" (272). The label "magician" is picked up by his peers to mark his special status. In the novel's last paragraph, Billy is still playing, headed for a pool room, "a place where even serious men sometimes go to seek the meaning of magical webs, mystical coin, golden birds, and other artifacts of the only cosmos in town."

"The only cosmos in town": the substitution of "cosmos" for the expected "game" suggests an important theme. Games are microcosmoses; the cosmos is a macrogame. Bowling and life are comparable: in both, chance and skill operate under arbitrary rules to produce winners and losers. Billy the gamesman is Billy the man. He plays his life as though the rules are meaningful, but the fact that local politicians—a couple of neighborhood guys like Patsy and Bindy McCall—can take away the home plate and close the ball park demonstrates that there are no absolute rules, no absolute meaning.

Billy does not grasp this existential conclusion; he only feels "the onset of mystery." When he returns home from the river, his intuition expresses itself in a dream: "He began to dream of tall buildings and thousands of dice and Kayo and Moon Mullins and their Uncle Willie all up in a palm tree, a scene which had great significance for the exhausted man, a significance which, as he reached for it, faded into the region where answers never come easy" (264). Billy's intimation of the meaning of life expresses itself through figures from a popular cartoon strip, a pile of dice (games), and tall buildings (the town). This is the anatomy of his location.

The novel's final phrase might be reversed: the town is Billy's only cosmos. Much earlier in the novel Billy thinks, "No town like Albany. . . . Billy couldn't imagine life outside Albany" (62). Billy is dislocated when he finds that *his* Albany actually belongs to the McCalls. The central dialectic occurs between the individual and the town. In two brief scenes (in chapters 9 and 13) Billy confronts the McCalls directly; his essential confrontation is the indirect one with the town that accepts the rule of the McCalls. Kennedy carefully re-creates the texture of this town. All the locations are presented concretely and correspond with the realities of Albany in 1938: streets, buildings, districts; bowling alleys, homes, bars. And the historical dimension, Albany's location in American time, is also accurately evoked, from the 1630 origins of Colonie Street to the nineteenth-century Albany of Bret Harte, Millard Fillmore, and Henry James to the recent Albany of Legs Diamond. This is Billy Phelan's cosmos.

Self-discovery takes place through two dialectical processes in *Billy Phelan's Greatest Game*. The first occurs between the individual and his town—Billy and Albany; the second occurs between the individual and his father—Billy and Francis Phelan and, as well, Martin and Edward Daugherty. Francis Phelan is a ghostly presence in the novel from the first chapter. There Martin Daugherty, seven or eight years younger than Billy's father, remembers Francis's involvement in two crucial moments: his killing a striking trolleyman in 1901 and his abandonment of his family in 1916. In the third chapter, Martin happens upon Francis in a bar and learns that the old man has returned to Albany to vote (twenty-one times) for the McCall ticket. Francis asks specifically about his own son and about Martin's father. Billy himself hears that his father is back in town from Bindy McCall, but doesn't actually meet him until chapter 15, when Billy posts a $400 bond to secure his father's release from jail. Arrested for his voting excess, Francis had called Martin, who then informed Billy.

As the three men sit in an Italian restaurant, it becomes clear that Billy has not simply recovered a father. Francis refuses to let Martin leave; he calls Billy "Bill." (Annie

Phelan corrects him on this in *Ironweed*.) Francis describes how his own father's death affected his life, but he seems unable to reenter his son's. He astonishes Billy by revealing that his departure in 1916 was precipitated by his accidental and fatal dropping of Billy's brother, Gerald. But for Billy, the most important moment occurs when he asks Francis for advice regarding the McCall demand that he inform on Morrie Berman. Francis recognizes the power of the McCalls and approves of spying for them. Billy simply rejects the advice: ''I look at it different'' (222), and he later expresses his disappointment to Martin Daugherty. Martin responds by recounting Francis's killing of the scab trolleyman in 1901: Francis has lived in a different world; the father cannot comprehend the son's dilemma. Billy remains existentially alone in his confrontation with the McCalls' Albany. (Billy has no son either, but in a significant exchange, his girlfriend, Angie Velez, briefly pretends to be pregnant and Billy must admit that he would acknowledge the child: ''he's got to know who his old man is'' [168].)

Other sons find different fathers. Bindy McCall's desperate desire to recover his son motivates the central action of the novel. Charlie Boy McCall is the privileged son of the powerful family. Morrie Berman, chief of the kidnappers, is the alienated son of Jake Berman, the radical tailor. Jake no longers speaks to his dissolute son, referring to him as ''a lead slug'' (115). Yet when Morrie is arrested for his part in the crime, Jake raises two thousand dollars for his defense. Billy expresses surprise: ''I thought old Jake didn't like Morrie'' (280). Jake doesn't, Martin confirms. But the father is bound to the son.

Martin Daugherty himself is the son most tied to his father and, as well, the father most tied to his son. Edward Daugherty is a senile playwright, exiled to a rest home; Peter Daugherty is a fourteen-year-old who has chosen to exile himself to a seminary (the "pederast priests" in Martin's view). Just as Billy's father was a professional player, Martin's father was a professional writer. Martin is a professional writer, too, but a journalist. He comments upon events; his father transformed events into art. Martin has published two nonfiction books and a volume of short stories, none of which he values, and he has a twelve-hundred-page manuscript in which he has tried to fictonalize and understand his father's life. (Although Kennedy's father may bear little resemblance to Martin's, Kennedy and Martin obviously have much in common: their journalism, their literary ambitions, their efforts to fictionalize and understand.) Edward Daugherty was a great writer, a playwright who dramatized the real occurrences of his lifetime, including Francis's 1901 trolley strike and, most notoriously, his own scandalous affair in 1908 with an actress, Melissa Spencer, and her lesbian lover, an affair which destroyed his career and the life of his wife, Katrina, Martin's mother.

In 1908, nineteen-year-old Melissa had been Edward Daugherty's lover; in 1913, Edward Daugherty composed his play, *The Flaming Corsage,* based on the affair. In 1928, a mature star of silent films, Melissa proposed to produce the play. After engaging in an intense three-day sexual encounter with her old lover's son, she obtained Edward's diary of the period from Martin. Now, in 1938, she has returned to Albany to star in a revival of the play. This time, aged forty-nine, she plays the role of Edward's wife, Katrina—she plays Martin's mother. And when Martin meets her in her hotel room, he consummates this complex oedipal drama with another sexual affair. (The episode is one of several in Kennedy's fiction in which the characters intentionally repeat significant moments from their past. Daniel Quinn's renewal of a liaison in "The Secrets of Creative Love" provides the clearest parallel.) Martin also recovers his father's ledger. Having had sex with his father's mistress and now, vicariously, with his father's wife, he symbolically retakes possession of his father.

His father has possessed him all along. Early in the novel, after noting Billy's fatherlessness from age nine, he realizes that his own problem is "similar but turned inside out: too much father, too much influence, too much fame, too much scandal, but also too much absence as the great man pursued his greatness" (44). Martin sees Billy's life as an exclamation point of self-assertion, his own as a question mark of self-doubt. Billy acts; Martin wonders. These are their essential roles in the novel. The recovery of the ledger has no practical effect, just as Billy's recovery of the derelict Francis has no practical effect on his predicament. When Martin visits his senile father at the novel's end, the old man cannot remember Melissa's last name, or anything else about her. He does not recognize the name of his grandson. For him, past and future have become equally meaningless. Morrie Berman and Charlie Boy McCall may lead useless lives, but they derive concrete support from their fathers; Billy and Martin do not, and this may be the source of their strength.

And yet the recovery of fathers is crucial to both Billy and Martin. It seems somehow to give them the confidence to defy the pressures of the McCalls' Albany, to assert their personal integrities against a corrupt town. It gives them a personal basis, a familial location, from which they can defy Albany. Billy clearly rebels; Martin deliberately defies the McCalls (and, as well, his own wife) by arranging to have his column on Billy published in Damon Runyon's column (his own paper having refused to offend the McCalls by printing it). And after his pointless conversation with his forgetful father, Martin completes a pattern of allusion in the novel by realizing "that all sons are Isaac, all fathers are Abraham, and that all Isaacs become Abrahams if they work at it long enough" (278).[5] To be sacrificed and to sacrifice is the lot of men in *Billy Phelan's Greatest Game*.

Martin is Billy turned inside out. There is a second important aspect to this truth: both are "magicians" of a sort. What luck is to Billy, precognition is to Martin. Billy plays games of chance; without conscious calculation he relies upon fortune. Martin, the thinker, is possessed of a peculiar intuition; he is, at times, able to foresee events—the suicide of a cousin, a thunderstorm, a three-horse parlay. His insights come in the form of crude imagery, and he regards himself as "a mystical naturalist" (24). Though he cannot explain his power, he prides himself upon it as one respect in which he excels his father. Significantly, the power left him in 1928, the year of his first encounter with Melissa, his father's former mistress, and is restored to him in 1938, the year of his second encounter with Melissa, who is now embodying his mother on stage. Kennedy does not, however, explain away precognition as some sort of psychological phenomenon: Daugherty's intuitions are genuine and verified. There is a real irrational dimension to the only cosmos in town.

Billy Phelan's Greatest Game represents Kennedy's successful attempt to portray men attempting to place themselves in their world. He re-creates the proletarian world of Depression Albany, a world in which men are especially vulnerable to displacement. The McCalls can dictate to Martin and his editor; Billy's lack of resources makes him even less likely to resist. A member of the *lumpenproletariat,* he seems to skate precariously on the thin ice of Albany's nighttown; neither a worker nor, apparently, a son, he seems to have no basis from which to defy the ostracism imposed on him. And yet, partly by identifying himself as his father's son, he discovers within himself the resource with which to locate a selfhood that is not dependent upon Albany. Martin, who has made his peace with Albany, must locate himself in the line of the Daughertys; he must accept as inevitable (Isaac and Abraham) the tensions which separate him from his father and from his son. Both victories are marginal ones. In the end Martin still cannot communicate with either his senile father or his alienated, Catholic son. The Billy who survives the night by the river is far from a triumphant self, even a triumphant *lumpenproletarian* self. But he has at least ceased to be a necessary Albanian; he can imagine an alternative. And so, when he returns to Albany's nighttown at the novel's end, he is still a thorough Albanian but, in an important sense, a freer one.

NOTES

1. Edward C. Reilly, "On an Averill Park Afternoon with William Kennedy," *The South Carolina Review* 21 (1989): 21.

2. See Reilly 14–15.

3. Larry McCaffery and Sinda Gregory, "An Interview with William Kennedy," *Alive and Writing* (Urbana: University of Illinois Press, 1987) 158.

Billy Phelan's Greatest Game

4. William Kennedy, *Billy Phelan's Greatest Game* (New York: Viking, 1978) 2. Subsequent references will be noted in parentheses.

5. For a discussion of the Isaac/Abraham conflict in the novel, see Daniel M. Murtaugh, "Fathers and Their Sons: William Kennedy's Hero-Transgressors," *Commonweal* 19 May 1989: 300.

CHAPTER SIX

Ironweed

Ironweed (1983) is in many ways the crucial novel in Kennedy's career as a writer. It is, of course, the best-seller which established him as a major voice in contemporary fiction, bringing him a wide audience and critical acclaim. It is the only one of his novels to have been filmed. Kennedy himself regards it as his "best book."[1] And it signals Kennedy's dedication to the project of centering his fiction on a hundred years in the lives of a group of Albany Irish families. *Ironweed* explores the vagrant life of Billy Phelan's father; the next novel, *Quinn's Book,* explores the life of Billy Phelan's brother-in-law's grandfather. The seminal work in this project is again the unpublished family chronicle, *The Angels and the Sparrows.* But as portions of the chronicle have been presented in the sequence of novels, Kennedy has expanded and altered the character and history of his protagonists. Francis Phelan, as he appears in the published novels, is a synthesis of his prototype in *The Angels and the Sparrows* and the figure of a bum from an unpublished nonfiction work called *The Lemon Weed.* Written in the 1960s, *The Lemon Weed* had been based on a series of articles on Albany's skid row written for the *Times-Union*.[2] Thus the authenticity of Francis's behavior and language derives from actual observations and encounters.

The Francis Phelan who appears briefly in three chapters of *Billy Phelan's Greatest Game* is an interesting derelict. He is endowed with a peculiar history—Martin Daugherty explains how he killed a strike-breaker in 1901 and he himself admits to having accidentally killed his second son, Gerald—and with a special vitality. But he is just a derelict, and is last seen in a drunken stupor beside his equally derelict "wife," Helen. In *Ironweed*, Francis is still an interesting derelict, but now the emphasis is upon the adjective, upon the peculiar history and the special vitality. The original Francis apparently lacked these qualities; Kennedy has reported that Francis in his original form was not even a baseball player.[3]

The action of *Ironweed* coincides with that of *Billy Phelan's Greatest Game* though the father and son only meet twice, once in each novel. Billy posts Francis's bail and accompanies him to a bar on Saturday, 22 October (*BPGG,* chap. 15; he *sees* Francis again later the same day but does not speak to him [*BPGG,* chap. 17]); and Francis finally visits his wife, son, and daughter at their home on Tuesday, 1 November (*Ironweed,* chap. 6). At the first encounter Francis promises to bring a turkey if he ever comes; in the second, he makes a point of bringing the turkey. In all other respects the two plots operate independently. It is worth establishing the two chronologies. (See chart on p. 82—the year is 1938.)

Two external factors play a role in dating the action of *Ironweed*. One is the religious calendar: October 31 is Halloween. This accounts for the costumed goblins who steal Helen's purse in chapter 3; it also casts a light on the

Date	*Billy Phelan's Greatest Game*	*Ironweed*
20 Oct Thu	Action begins (chap. 1)	
21 Fri	Billy is ostracized (13)	
22 Sat	Billy meets Francis (15)	
24 Mon	Charlie Boy released (19)	
25 Tues	Daugherty writes column (19)	
31 Mon		Action begins (1)
1 Nov Tues	Column published; Billy	Helen dies (5);
	restored (19)	Francis returns home (6)
2 Wed		Early morning: Francis
		kills Legionnaire; Rudy
		dies; Francis departs and
		returns (7)

ghosts from his past who come to haunt Francis. November 1 is All Saints Day, the day the church glorifies God for all his saints, known and unknown; and November 2 is All Souls Day, the day the church prays for the souls of the faithful who are suffering in purgatory. All of the souls in *Ironweed* seem to be suffering; Albany is their purgatory. Francis Phelan is far from his saintly namesake in his piety; his three stigmata—his truncated nose and index finger and his limp—derive from drunken brawls, not beatific ecstasies. Still, like St. Francis, Francis Phelan does live a vagrant life, and though he does not speak to animals, he does converse with the dead. The second external aspect of the dating of *Ironweed* lies in the famous incident of 30 October 1938: Orson Welles's famous broadcast of *The War of the Worlds*. The event is referred to several times; it ties the action to history, and it makes an oblique commentary upon the psychological environment of the Great Depression: the paranoia which led people to panic at the prospect of a Martian invasion may be related to the paranoia which led the Legionnaires to fear the dispossessed and to rampage through the hobo jungle at the novel's end.

Numerous narrative details connect *Ironweed* with its predecessor. The major events of Francis's life were sketched in *Billy Phelan's Greatest Game:* his involvement in the 1901 trolley strike which culminated in his killing the scab brakeman with a stone; his abandonment of his family in 1916; his return to Albany in 1938 to vote (twenty-one times) for the McCall ticket, leading to his arrest and Billy's posting of bail. The major events of Billy's recent troubles are alluded to in *Ironweed:* Helen reads Martin Daugherty's column in the *Times-Union* on Billy and the kidnapping. Billy receives a phone call informing him that his ban has been rescinded in *Ironweed* (chapter 6); in *Billy Phelan's Greatest Game* this moment of restoration occurs offstage, between chapters 19 and 20. A minor but typical link between the two narratives occurs in the first chapter of *Ironweed* as Francis walks through the St. Agnes Cemetery. He notices the recent grave of Louis (Big Daddy) Dugan, the pool hustler who played a small role in *Billy Phelan's Greatest Game,* dying in chapter 17 of that novel. Marcus Gorman's brief mention in *Ironweed*—he charges Francis fifty dollars to defend him against the election fraud charges—ties *Ironweed* to *Legs* as well as to *Billy Phelan's Greatest Game.*

But although *Ironweed* and *Billy Phelan's Greatest Game* occupy the same time and place, there are important differences in their treatment of theme and in their tone. Although both novels describe dislocated lives, the dislocations are different in cause and in consequence.

Billy Phelan's alienation is virtually imposed upon him. His decision not to act—not to spy on Morrie Berman—leads to Albany's withdrawal from Billy. Without leaving his place he discovers himself out of place; on instructions from the McCalls, Albany has abruptly ceased to be his Albany. And then, before he can fully comprehend his situation, he finds himself relocated: through the intervention of Martin Daugherty his place is restored to him.

Francis Phelan has elected dislocation. But just as Billy's alienation is partly the consequence of his own choice, so Francis's alienation is partly due to circumstances. In 1901, aged twenty-one, he found himself at the forefront of a demonstration against strike-breaking trolley operators. The situation was a volatile one, and it had been created by the trolley company and the larger economic pressures of American society in the early twentieth century, but Francis's throwing of the stone which fatally cracks the skull of the scab, Harold Allen, remains an action for which he must assume primary responsibility. He is more the actor than the victim. Having killed the man, Francis fled Albany until assured that the authorities had not identified him. During this first exile, he joined a professional baseball team in Dayton, Ohio, and so, every spring and summer thereafter, he abandoned Albany and his family for the seasonal exile of the baseball season (finally playing three seasons as a third baseman with the major league Washington Senators).

Francis's major dislocation—his twenty-two-year absence from Albany and family—is also primarily the result of his own action. On 26 April 1916, having had a few beers on the way home, he let his thirteen-day-old son slip through his diaper and fall to his death on the kitchen floor. He was not drunk; the event was a genuine accident, but Francis cannot face his Albany—his wife, relatives, and neighbors—and flees into the vagrant life which leads downward to his derelict condition as the novel opens in October 1938. Eventually he is driven to return and replace himself in Albany, an act of courage and integrity. He finds that just as it never knew who killed Harold Allen, Albany never learned who killed Gerald Phelan: his wife, Annie, never told anyone. Nonetheless, Francis discovers in the Albany of 1938 a sort of pentimento. All his Albanies are present in this Albany— present in the form of vivid memories, such as his recollection of his sexual initiation with Katrina Daugherty, Martin's mother; in the form of the voices of the dead, as in his graveyard conversation with Gerald; or in the form of the ghosts that haunt him on the streetcars and in the backyards of Albany: the ghosts of Harold Allen, the scab; Aldo Campione, the horse thief who was killed by the police as he tried to leap into Francis's boxcar; Dick Doolan (Rowdy Dick), a bum whom Francis killed in self-defense; Fiddler Quain, who had joined Francis at the barricade in 1901; Strawberry Bill, with whom Francis fled Albany in 1916. Francis's Albany is haunted by the Albanies of Francis's past.

This haunted quality distinguishes Francis from Billy. Francis has lived a long and violent life. Now, aged fifty-eight, he returns to Albany and begins to make sense of his life. For the first time he acquires an "insight into a pattern, an overview of all the violence in his history, of how many had died or been maimed by his hand, or who had died . . . as an indirect result of his violent ways."[4] The ghosts of these men travel with him on the Albany trolleys or stand outside the Albany windows he stares through. Eventually they gather—forty-three of them—in bleachers which they have erected in the backyard of his family's Third Street home, and Francis tries to dismiss them: "You're all dead, and if you ain't, you oughta be. I'm the one is livin'. I'm the one puts you on the map" (177). They exist, he realizes, because he perceives them.

Recollection plays as important a role in *Ironweed* as it did in *Legs,* but whereas Jack Diamond's survivors recall him as a puzzle and a source of anecdotes (and Jack himself in his lifetime takes a similar approach as he recalls his own past), *Ironweed* consists largely of Francis Phelan's own, very undetached recollection of the events which comprise the pattern of his violent life. Marcus Gorman tries to solve the problem of Jack Diamond forty-three years after Jack's death; Francis Phelan must solve the pressing problem of himself before he dies. The ghosts which haunt him on Halloween 1938 are part of the problem. They are not dead; the "map" they have been put on is the map of Francis's life, and he cannot simply dismiss them. They will not disappear; the "many" who died directly or indirectly by his actions are not possessions which he can cast off; they possess him. Their final gesture in the backyard is to chant the *Dies Irae,* the hymn from the requiem mass which describes the Day of Judgment and prays for mercy.

The ghosts of these men belong to the violent pattern of his past life; Francis is also possessed by benign visions of the women, past and present, who represent a redemptive element in his life: Katrina Daugherty, the woman who initiated him in 1897; Annie Farrell, the woman who married him in 1898; Helen Archer, the woman who has lived with him since 1929. Francis has never abused women. After leaving the family home with its bleachers of men, Francis goes to a flophouse where he briefly encounters a parallel vison of women: "In a corner of the room Francis saw three long-skirted women who became four who became three and then four again" (195). He does not immediately recognize them, but soon they assume "the faces of all the women Francis had ever known" (202). At one point they become his Fates: his mother as Clotho, crocheting a sampler; Katrina as Lachesis, measuring the cloth; and Helen as Atropos, snipping the threads. "Then they all became Annie" (202).

Katrina Daugherty died in a fire in 1912. But passing her house on Rosskam's junk wagon, Francis re-creates his peculiar romantic episode with her in July 1897. The interlude is complicated by the memory of the unconcealed hatred Francis's mother, Kathryn, bore for her neighbor. This affair between seventeen-year-old Francis and the middle-aged Katrina (mother of nine-year-old Martin Daugherty) has a odd lyrical quality about it. She plucks him from the tree he is trimming, seduces him, and rhapsodizes about "my beautiful Adonis of Arbor Hill" (110). The Francis who recalls the forty-one-year-old affair is a hardened, mutilated bum, but he still contains within him the naïve youth who fell under the spell of Katrina's body and her rhetoric. Katrina represents Francis's initiation into the mystery of womanhood. (Kennedy has confessed, "I *love* Katrina," and has suggested that ever since finishing *Ironweed* he has contemplated a novel focusing upon Katrina and her relationship with her husband, Edward, and his mistress, Melissa Spencer.[5])

Annie embodies the fulfillment of womanhood and the home which Francis abandoned but never lost. She has kept silent about his having killed his son; she has rejected all other men; she immediately welcomes him upon his unexpected return. (Peg, his daughter, initially resents him, but then she too forgives and embraces him.) Annie has preserved the physical remnants of his past in a trunk in the attic ("this aerie of reconstitutable time" [169]). And so she presides over Francis's recentering of his life. He takes from the trunk a 1916 suit and dresses himself as he was. The moment is in some ways comparable to Martin Daugherty's resumption after ten years of his affair with Melissa Spencer in *Billy Phelan's Greatest Game*. But Francis's reconstitution of his past is entirely domestic in character; it marks a renewal of his place in his family.

Francis takes out his third baseman's glove and passes it on to his son, Billy; he takes a baseball autographed by Ty Cobb and passes it on to his grandson, Daniel Quinn; he takes a 1910 letter from his daughter, Peg, and uses it to reconnect himself with her. Reclaiming and dispensing these traces of his past, he relocates himself in the continuity of his family. Despite Annie's invitation, however, he cannot yet translate this emotional relocation into a physical one. He cannot accept her offer of a permanent refuge from the world he has known. In his world of violence he has never forgotten the world of Annie's Albany: "I went my whole life rememberin' things here that were like nothin' I ever saw anywhere" (163). But, as the men in the bleachers remind him, neither can he forget the world of violence. When he leaves Annie, he rejoins his bum friend, Rudy, and sets off in search of Helen and other bums.

Helen is the final important woman in Francis's life, and she is in many ways his foil. She too is a bum, a dislocated person, a returning exile. But her history has a melodramatic quality that contrasts with Francis's extraordinary but naturalistic drama. She is the daughter of an upper-middle-class Albany family whose father dissipated the family fortune and committed suicide by leaping off the same viaduct that Georgie Fox leapt from in *Billy Phelan's Greatest Game*. Her mother subverted Helen's father's will by devoting the remainder of the estate to ensuring that Helen's brother graduate from law school, thus compelling Helen to abandon her dreams of becoming a concert pianist and to withdraw from Vassar. She worked in a music shop where she was seduced and then cast off by the shop owner. When she finally discovered her mother's duplicity over the will, she repudiated her family absolutely. Eventually she met Francis Phelan, lived with him as his wife, suffered a miscarriage, and accompanied him in a descent into vagrancy. She, unlike Francis, has retained her dogmatic Catholicism, firmly rejecting the Protestant salvation preached by Reverend Chester. Francis drinks the Reverend's soup and coaxes a pair of the Reverend's socks; still, despite his nine years with Helen, Francis's residual Catholicism allows him to recognize only one wife—Annie.

Helen's specific alienation from her mother is similar to Francis's: in *Billy Phelan's Greatest Game,* sons need their absent fathers; in *Ironweed,* sons and daughters must escape narrow-minded and deceitful mothers. Kathryn Phelan had been an unhappy, hateful woman deformed by her distorted Catholic pieties, a "denier of life" (90); she had scattered salt on the roots of Katrina Daugherty's tree; she had opposed Francis's marriage to Annie, and Francis had consequently refused to enter her house. Helen has the satisfaction of learning that in the end her favored brother callously assigned their mother to a poorhouse. More generally, Helen is, like Francis, an alienated Albanian; but unlike Francis, she cannot relocate herself in Albany. She cannot reconnect herself with her brother, now a prominent political lawyer. And as Francis is recovering himself in the attic trunk and distributing his memories to his heirs, Helen, who bears a cancerous tumor, not children, is dying alone in Palumbo's Hotel, hearing the music that represents the life she has not led. Knowing that Francis is drawn to returning to his wife, she consciously chooses to sacrifice herself by departing from his life. She passes up their planned reunion at the mission and goes to the hotel where she has chosen to die. After he finds her there dead, Francis recalls her saying, "All I want in the world is to have my name put back among the family" (223). Francis imagines fulfilling her wish by someday returning to her grave and erecting a memorial stone.

Helen's wish is, of course, Francis's achievement: he does have his name put back among his family. (He is especially pleased to learn that Annie has purchased a place for him in the family cemetery plot.) This is his great victory. In the novel's opening chapter Francis walks among the family graves in the St. Agnes Cemetery and thinks, "Being dead here would situate a man in place and time" (13). Both Francis and Helen want to situate themselves permanently in place and time, but Helen does not succeed. She too has roots in Albany, and in some respects she is as tough a weed as Francis. But her memories remain sentimental, especially as she approaches her death. When Francis tells her he has conversed with his dead son, she responds, "We shouldn't be here. We should go someplace else." And Francis agrees: "Right. That's where we oughta go. Else" (64). But for both of them, there is only Albany; there is no "someplace else."

Francis's conversation with Gerald, whose death precipitated his exile, marks the beginning of his relocation of himself in Albany. Helen's inability to speak with her brother—or, indeed, to speak seriously with anyone other than Francis—condemns her to her final isolation and death.

The importance of one's family name runs as a motif throughout the novel. Francis insists to Rudy that Helen has no last name, and he identifies Sandra as "Sandra There-ain't-no-more. She's only got one name, like Helen" (30). However, when Helen briefly recovers her identify as a performer—singing "My Pal" at The Gilded Cage—Francis gives her her full name, Helen Archer. When Sandra dies, frozen to death outside the mission, she has not achieved an individual identity. When even Peewee doesn't know her name, Francis observes, "Don't make much difference now" (62). And in the end, after carrying Rudy's body to Memorial Hospital, Francis gives the nameless bum a last name—Newton. The name is ironic, a play upon Rudy's eccentric questions and answers—"He knew where the Milky Way was" (221)—but it does situate him in place and time. Lest the relevance of the date, All Saints Day, escape the reader, young Daniel Quinn, Peg's boy, informs Francis that he has just learned that "it's the day we remember the martyrs who died for faith and nobody knows their names" (165). Sandra and Rudy and Helen cannot be said to have died for the faith, but they are unknown martyrs of a sort. Francis's response to Daniel must be read at two levels: "Oh yeah. . . . I remember them fellas." He remembers having learned about martyrs of the past during his own schooldays; he has also known the martyrs of his lifetime—the Strawberry Bill Bensons, the Aldo Campiones, the Sandras, the Helen Archers, martyrs who will not be buried in family plots.

Francis Phelan, bum, is not an obvious avatar of Jack Diamond, gangster; but in important respects they are similar. They are Kennedy heroes: Irish-Catholic rebels who posit their values and styles of living—very different styles of living—against the ways of the world. But there is a revealing parallel not shared by the other Kennedy heroes. They are men with two women, one a good (or would-be good) Irish-Catholic wife, the other a reprobate Irish-Catholic mistress with (quite different) musical ambitions. The finesse with which Jack managed to balance the needs of both women was one of the clearest measures of his inimitable style. Francis lacks finesse. He never resolves his dual loyalties (he *has* loyalties); Helen effectively solves his problem by dying. Francis never achieves in his life the balance which Marcus Gorman so envied in Jack's.

At the end of the novel, in his fullest moment of self-understanding, Francis realizes exactly this defect: "He felt certain now that he would never attain the balance that allowed so many other men to live peaceful, nonviolent, nonfugitive lives" (215). Of course, balanced Jack Diamond lived a violent, fugitive life: his triumph lay in maintaining a tense balance of destructive forces, an increasingly desperate balance that is finally upset and leads to his assassination. Bailey did not need balance; he pursued his zany course six inches above the ground of an unbalanced Albany. Billy Phelan is always balanced—in games of chance and love; a combination of luck and poise preserve him. His problem occurs when the playing field tilts beneath him. Francis does not choose violence the way Jack Diamond did; the catastrophes of his life are the result of circumstances, not policy. Unlike Bailey, he walks on the hard ground of Depression Albany; real stones break real skulls. And the circumstances of Francis's life, unlike those of Billy's, have often placed a stone in his hand and a skull in his way.

But Francis correctly perceives that the source of his imbalance is in some degree internal; he cannot simply blame circumstances. He analyzes himself further: "He believed he was a creature of unknown and unknowable qualities, a man in whom there would never be an equanimity of both impulsive and premeditated action." And he concludes: "My guilt is all that I have left. If I lose it, I have stood for nothing, done nothing, been nothing" (216). Francis's sense of his guilt defines him as a man and a hero. Gerald, the wise, dead infant, knows this; Helen, as she prepares to die, knows this. Others forget or misremember, do not judge themselves or misjudge; Francis remembers and judges.

And immediately following Francis's recognition of the internal motive which has driven him, the external cycle of violence and flight renews itself, and circumstances seem to drive him again into centrifugal flight. The American Legionnaires charge through the hobo encampment, burning the jerry-built structures and beating the unfortunate inhabitants. When one fatally cracks Rudy's skull with a baseball bat, Francis instinctively responds in kind, breaking the killer's back. In 1901 his baseball throwing skill did in Harold Allen; in 1938 his baseball hitting skill does in the Legionnaire: "Francis connected with a stroke that would have sent any pitch over any center-field fence in any ball park anywhere" (216). The fatal consequences of his third baseman's skills frame his Albany experience.

Francis bears the dying Rudy to the hospital, and then must flee again.

His final flight and return, occupying the last seven pages of the narrative, are deliberately set in a conditional mode: "It would be three-fifteen by the clock on the First Church when Francis headed south toward Palumbo's Hotel. . . . He would walk past Palumbo's nightman. . . . He would see light coming out from under the door" (221). Kennedy has claimed that his purpose was not to render the action "hypothetical," but rather to indicate that this is an "overview" of the last moments of Francis's story. Everything that happens is, Kennedy asserts, "real."[6] Francis discovers Helen's body in the room at Palumbo's. In a repetition of his flight from the killing of Gerald in 1916, he boards a freight train running south. During his day at the St. Agnes cemetery, Francis had remembered that in 1916 he had shared the southbound freight with Strawberry Bill, a bum who died a week after they reached New York City. Now, in his current flight, he is joined by the ghost of Strawberry Bill, a ghost come not to remind him of the violent episodes of his past, but to lead him to leap off the train and return to Annie's attic, where, as the novel ends, he waits to see whether he has been identified as the killer of the Legionnaire. If not, he has before him the prospect of a cot in his grandson's room, a symbol of his reintegration into the line of his family. "It was a mighty nice little room" (227). The happiness is contingent; Francis cannot be sure he had not been identified, but with this happy, domestic vision, the novel and Francis Phelan's "violent ways" come to an end.

Despite this hopeful note, the tone of *Ironweed* is considerably darker than that of *Billy Phelan's Greatest*

Game. The coldness of Depression Albany is much more clearly felt in the second novel. Billy spends the night of 22 October freezing beside the Hudson, but except for this catharsis, he (and Martin Daugherty as well) is usually found indoors. The games he plays are indoor games—bowling, pool, poker. Francis played outdoors—baseball. And as a derelict he has spent much of the last twenty-two years on the road and in the weeds. Nearly all of his memories are outdoor memories: up in a tree, watching Katrina Daugherty; on the streets of Albany, stopping the trolley; underneath a bridge, defending his shoes from the grasp of Rowdy Dick Doolan. And he spends most of his days and nights in *Ironweed* in a cold Albany. He is first seen working in the cemetery; he and Rudy and Helen walk the streets until he eventually deposits Helen in the abandoned car occupied by Finny; he himself sleeps the night of the thirty-first in the weeds. The next day, he works the streets with the junkman, Rosskam. That night he intends to spend around the fire in the hobo jungle, but the assault of the Legionnaires drives him to the freight car headed south.

It is deadly cold in Albany. Sandra freezes to death outside the Holy Redemption Mission, and her corpse is chewed by dogs. The coldness is emphasized by the desperate efforts of various characters to escape it. Helen's acceptance of the slight shelter of Finny's car makes the point. Although much of the action of the novel does indeed take place indoors, these scenes are explicitly islands surrounded by the pervasive cold. They are temporary and inadequate refuges. The first of these is the Mission of Holy Redemption, where Francis and Rudy meet Helen after their day in the graveyard. The mission represents society's pious and inadequate offering to the dislocated.

It is maintained by the Methodist Church, not the state, and is operated by the moralistic Reverend Chester, who kindly gives the sober Francis a pair of warm socks but who remorselessly expels a backsliding Little Red into the cold. The Reverend also excludes Sandra, and as the city's ambulance won't assist her either, she freezes.

The next refuge Francis and Helen visit is The Gilded Cage. Francis has known the singing barman, and they reminisce over beers. Helen has her moment of recapturing a fantasized past as a performer, and then the bar closes and they return to the cold. The next refuge is Jack's place, where Helen had spent the previous night. This night, however, their reception is less warm, and after a glass of wine they again find themselves in the cold. From this point their paths diverge, and they find significantly different escapes from the cold.

Helen stays as long as she can bear it in Finny's car, then visits a series of temporary refuges: St. Anthony's Church, where she hears the All Saints mass; the Waldorf Cafeteria, where she cannot retain her fifteen-cent toast and coffee; the Pruyn Library, where she reads Martin Daugherty's column on Billy; the Modern Music Shop, where she steals a recording of Beethoven's Ninth Symphony; and finally Palumbo's Hotel, where she pays $2.50 for two nights, in case she doesn't die the first day. Helen's sequence of inherently impermanent refuges reflects her inevitable decline to her death.

Francis moves in a different direction. His night in the weeds may have been—if he has not been identified as a killer—his last cold night. After his memory-filled day with Rosskam he returns home and reconciles himself with Annie, Billy, Peg, and young Daniel. But believing he would never "fit in," he then attempts to return to his vagrant life; he does not know that Helen is dead, and he expects to rejoin her and Rudy. Francis tries to resume his derelict life in the flophouse, the hobo jungle, Palumbo's, and the freight car; each proves to be a closed exit. Helen and Rudy die. In the end Francis returns to the attic. There he enjoys at least the prospect of a permanent refuge from the cold.

The classical allusions embedded in *Ironweed* have received notice.[7] In the fullest treatment of Kennedy's use of classical sources Michael Tierce has argued that the novel is as carefully structured upon the archetype of Homer's *Odyssey* as was Joyce's *Ulysses*.[8] Some of the parallels may be overstated, but Kennedy evidently did have Homer and Joyce in mind as he wrote. Tierce argues, for example, that the first chapter, set in St. Agnes Cemetery, reflects elements of Odysseus's experience in Hades; that Reverend Chester of the Mission of Holy Redemption is an echo of Circe; that Helen's pathetic song in The Gilded Cage connects the episode with Homer's sirens. Such a pattern of allusions indicates that the design of *Ironweed* is far from naïve.

The title *Ironweed* is explained in an excerpt adapted from an entry in the Audubon Society's *Field Guide to North American Wildflowers* prefixed to the novel. The key sentence is the last: "The name refers to the toughness of the stem." "The stem" suggests the genetic source of Francis's resilience, the toughness bred into his Irish-American strain. Francis himself adopts the image when, in an episode in the middle of the novel, he imagaines his own conception and birth. He sees his "soulish body" develop in his mother's womb until it reached the form of an infant. Then his father "yanked" it free "and swiftly molded him into a bestial weed" which then "sprouted" into the Francis Phelan who now envisions the sprouting (99). The weediness of Francis and his father is their virtue. It is the virtue of most of the Phelans and Daughertys and Quinns and Farrells. Only the mother from whom Francis was yanked is exempt. In chapter 1, Kathryn Phelan is depicted in her grave, bitterly weaving dead weeds into crosses and eating them with "an insatiable revulsion" (2)—an apt symbol of her devouring piety. But though she too has a perverted toughness, even she cannot weave or consume her son. Francis is the Ironweed; he survives everything.

Ironweed was filmed in 1987 (directed by Hector Babenco). Kennedy wrote the screenplay, and, with his wife, makes a cameo appearance in the scene at Oscar Reo's Gilded Cage in which Helen (Meryl Streep) sings "He's My Pal." The film version is especially worth noting because Kennedy involved himself in the production and assisted in identifying the location of authentic scenes in the Albany area. The film's images of Francis Phelan's world—one of its particular strengths—thus reflect Kennedy's sense of the place.

NOTES

1. Kay Bonetti, "An Interview with William Kennedy," *The Missouri Review* 8 (1985): 72.

2. Michael Robertson, "The Reporter as Novelist," *Columbia Journalism Review* 24 (1985–86): 52.

3. Larry McCaffery and Sinda Gregory, "An Interview with William Kennedy," *Alive and Writing* (Urbana: University of Illinois Press, 1987) 173.

4. William Kennedy, *Ironweed* (New York: Viking, 1983) 145. Subsequent references will be noted in parentheses.

5. Edward C. Reilly, "On an Averill Park Afternoon with William Kennedy," *The South Carolina Review* 21 (1989): 20.

6. Kay Bonetti, "An Interview with William Kennedy," *The Missouri Review* 8 (1985): 82. Daniel Murtaugh, in "Fathers and Their

Sons'' (*Commonweal* 19 May 1989: 302), offers a plausible reading of the ending as "merely a dream."

7. See Peter P. Clarke, "Classical Myth in William Kennedy's *Iron-weed*," *Critique* 27 (1986): 177–84, and Daniel M. Murtaugh, "Fathers and Their Sons: William Kennedy's Hero-Transgressors," *Commonweal* 19 May 1989: 301–02.

8. Michael Tierce, "William Kennedy's Odyssey: The Travels of Francis Phelan," *Classical and Modern Literature* 8 (1988): 247–63.

CHAPTER SEVEN

Quinn's Book

The first important shift in the character of Kennedy's fiction appeared in 1975 as he dropped the setting of his second narrative a crucial half foot. *The Ink Truck* had been an extravagant fable set, as Kennedy said, "six inches off the ground" of a pseudo-Albany; *Legs* was a plausible reconstruction of a history firmly placed on the surface of 1930s Albany, an actuality verified by extensive research and personal memories of Kennedy's own relatives. Bailey's experience in *The Ink Truck* was presented objectively as a sequence of arbitrary and bizarre events; Jack Diamond's experience in *Legs* was presented as a complex series of dialectics: between the gangster and others, between the gangster and himself, between the present and the remembered past. *Billy Phelan's Greatest Game* and *Ironweed* developed the new approach: their narratives were set in the concrete past of 1930s Albany, and their characters were defined through their relationships with others and with their own pasts.

Though Kennedy has specifically disavowed the application of "trilogy" to the three novels—*Legs, Billy Phelan's Greatest Game*, and *Ironweed*—they do thus possess a coherence that distinguishes them from the novels that precede and follow them, and this is more than a matter of their shared characters or even of their shared time frame. Though none of their protagonists is actually a worker, all three books may be loosely classified as proletarian novels. That is, they present the experience of lower-class characters (or of middle-class characters like Marcus Gorman and Martin Daugherty, who have emerged from the ethnic environment of the lower class and who can identify with it). These characters inhabit a Darwinian world where survival depends upon successful response to immediate economic and political pressures. They make choices, but always in contexts that prohibit long-range considerations. They cannot, any of them, plan for the future. Jack Diamond deals with a succession of crises, epitomized by the sequence of assassination attempts; Marcus Gorman quickly abandons his ambition for eventual political office; Billy rolls from game to game, wager to wager; Martin Daugherty deals with the abuses of the machine on an instance by instance basis; Francis and Helen strive to make it from one meal to the next. All of them are, in some respects, hard-boiled characters, though Kennedy's persistent strain of lyrical mysticism, exemplified in the two voices of Francis Phelan, prevents any of them from being merely a contemporary variation on the 1930s hard-boiled type.

In *Quinn's Book* (1988) Kennedy makes the second dramatic shift in the orientation of his fiction. In some respects it is a shift backward (and upward); its narrative lifts off again like that of *The Ink Truck*. Daniel Quinn has much the same autonomy that Bailey had. He confronts a world of conflicts, but he never finds himself limited by immediate necessity; he is not bound to pedestrian reality.

Bailey was a lucky striker, not, apparently, troubled by the need to pay for meals or mortgages. Daniel Quinn is a lucky orphan. He meets a series of fascinating personalities, and he encounters no serious obstacles to his precocious determination to be a writer and a lover. He, a poor Irish orphan, is readily adopted by a Dutch dowager; before the midpoint of the novel he receives a fifteen-year endowment from the dowager's son. Most tellingly, he does not even need the endowment. Though catastrophes punctuate his life, he is never troubled by the dull economic necessities faced daily by his twentieth-century proletarian descendants. The dislocations of Bailey and Daniel Quinn are of a different quality from those of the "trilogy" heroes.

Quinn's Book is characterized by rhetorical excess and an extravagant, melodramatic plot in which a sequence of calamities press upon one another: floods and fires, deaths and resurrections, riots and wars, secret societies and underground railroads, romances and ghostly voices all crowd the action. The scene is specifically Albany, but the surplus of incident tends to overwhelm the particularities of the setting. Quinn, like Bailey, finds himself in a puzzling world, but the puzzles lack the human, psychological complexities of those encountered by Diamond and Gorman, Billy and Martin, Francis and Helen. In *Quinn's Book* the poetics of memory and place give way to a rhetoric of social observation. The principal difficulties of Quinn's world—matters such as the treatment of immigrants, slaves, workers, and soldiers—are presented as sociological phenomena. *Quinn's Book* offers a largely objective panorama of a world full of representative figures and situations. Its main characters tend to be engaged with History and Society and the Meaning of Life and

Love; its minor characters tend to be Typical People—the Black Slave, the Irish Worker, the Dutch Dowager, the Yankee Industrialist.

Another way of defining the difference is to note the novel's humor. Kennedy has said that, inspired by writers like Damon Runyon and Ben Hecht, his earliest literary ambitions included the desire "to make people laugh." He has pointed out that even *Ironweed,* for all its depressing elements, contains "all of that kind of crazy bum dialogue that lifts the novel into a realm of wackiness, a bumdom that is very comic."[1] And there is indeed a wry humor in some of Francis Phelan's self-evaluations and an absurd comedy in the nonsequitors of his conversations with Rudy. Similarly, there are comic moments in *Legs*—most memorably in the episode with the German playwright Weissberg—and in *Billy Phelan's Greatest Game.* But the burden of these novels is serious. The protagonists strive and suffer. Most of the comedy is verbal; the characters use humor as a way of expressing a momentary exuberance. Their world is not funny, but by making fun of it, they can assert their independence from it.

Quinn's world too is full of suffering; its disasters—natural and human—are far more catastrophic than those of the earlier novels; still, Kennedy is correct to observe that "there's a world of humor in *Quinn's Book.*"[2] But the comedy here, like that in *The Ink Truck,* is often situational, even slapstick. A pretentious socialite is punished by being publicly stripped and spanked on her pimply bottom. A rapping spirit from the other world embarrasses an actress by tapping forty-one times in response to a question concerning her age. Quinn manages to preserve the enigmatic disk that comprises his inheritance from his father by playing a Tom Sawyerish deception on a bully, tricking him into stealing a worthless shovel. Quinn is an earnest boy and then an earnest man. Yet his most serious discoveries often emerge in absurd contexts. As children he and Maud realize they are meant for one another as they secretly (and attentively) observe John the Brawn copulating alternately with an apparent corpse and a wealthy dowager. That the copulation results in the resurrection of the corpse adds to the grotesque comedy of the situation. The humor of Quinn's world is as extravagant as its violence.

Kennedy has not, however, merely returned to his radical/dadaist origins after a two-decade naturalistic interlude with Legs Diamond and the Phelans. *Quinn's Book* is explicitly a continuation of the project announced in *Billy Phelan's Greatest Game*. The protagonist, Daniel Quinn, is the direct ancestor of the young Daniel Quinn (Billy Phelan's nephew and Francis Phelan's grandson) born almost a century later; Emmett Daugherty, the senior Daniel Quinn's occasional adviser, is the grandfather of Billy and Francis's friend, Martin Daugherty. (Emmett's account of his arrival in Albany had been recalled by Francis Phelan near the end of *Ironweed*.) *Quinn's Book* thus extends the Phelan-Quinn-Daugherty saga backward to the mid-nineteenth-century emigration of the Irish-Americans to Albany, drawing upon another portion of the unpublished *Angels and the Sparrows*.

Although Kennedy has carefully researched every detail of his portrait of life in nineteenth-century Albany, he has not been satisfied to paint a genre piece. Instead, he has elected to involve the progenitors of his family chronicle in a swirling historical action that treats Albany, perhaps too insistently, as a microcosm of antebellum and Civil War America. The resulting fiction, a Baileyesque farrago involving Phelan, Quinn, and Daugherty progenitors, thus represents a new departure for Kennedy—and a commendable one in view of the obvious temptation merely to repeat himself after the celebrations of *Ironweed*. Indeed, Kennedy's first intention had been to depart even further from precedent: "My new novel, *Quinn's Book,* originally started out in Germany and then moved to Albany. But that didn't work."[3] No trace of the German origins remains in the published novel, though the short stories "An Exchange of Gifts" and "The Secrets of Creative Love" do allude to the German experiences of the twentieth-century Daniel Quinn, great-grandson of the novel's hero. Kennedy's second plan was to employ "interlocking chapters set in alternate centuries."[4] This too proved unsatisfactory, and Kennedy resolved upon the final design, abandoning the twentieth-century chapters and setting the novel entirely in the Albany of the middle decades of the nineteenth century.

The result was generally praised by critics; T. Coraghessan Boyle said it confirmed that Kennedy was "unparalleled among his contemporaries" as a writer of historical fiction.[5] Most critics shared Boyle's enthusiasm (several also shared his minor reservations: that Kennedy's adoption of a nineteenth-century rhetorical voice sometimes seems to slip, and that occasionally the weight of historical incident obscures the narrative progress[6]). In the context of the Albany cycle *Quinn's Book* is unquestionably a major achievement. It adds crucial new dimensions to Kennedy's portrayal of the paradigmatic Irish-American experience of America.

In addition to providing a historical foundation for the lives of his later heroes, the new novel can also claim a thematic continuity with the earlier novels. The central problem of *Quinn's Book* again presents itself in terms of location and dislocation, but now location is defined less in terms of concrete social pressures and predicaments and more in terms of a nexus of historical forces. The distinction is not absolute. The social situations confronted by Legs, Billy, and Francis were certainly historically conditioned; matters such as Prohibition and the Great Depression manifested themselves in details of scene and behavior throughout these novels. But Billy, for example, never thinks of himself or his problems as somehow caused by or typical of his times. Billy lives the Depression; he does not confront it.

Daniel Quinn confronts his time. He deliberately faces the larger issues of mid-century America. Some of these—such as the passing of the Dutch hegemony—are specific to Albany; others reflect broader concerns—the operations of industrial capitalism, the sometimes contentious assimilation of immigrant labor, the problem of race slavery, the Civil War. Daniel Quinn must place himself amid these dynamic historical changes. He cannot, as Jack Diamond and Billy and Francis Phelan could, define himself by rejecting his given place as an Irish-American. He has been given nothing (except that enigmatic Celtic disk). He is an utterly new American—a new Albanian: as an immigrant and an orphan he is less dislocated than unlocated. He is the nineteenth-century boy protagonist, a David Copperfield uncertain of whether he will be the hero of his own story. Unlike the English boy, however, the young Albanian inhabits a violent, unstable world that provides few secure standards of behavior. David Copperfield at least knew what it meant to be a hero—a gentleman.

Quinn's Book

Daniel Quinn must invent what he wants to be (principally, a journalist and a lover). *Quinn's Book,* therefore, is much less retrospective than *Legs, Billy Phelan's Greatest Game,* or *Ironweed.* It is prospective, emphasizing the choices Daniel Quinn makes regarding his future. Although he is more defined by his past than Bailey was, he is cast in Bailey's mold as someone whose existence is measured by his choices. Some of these are personal—to write, to love; some are social and ideological—to oppose slavery and war. When, as a boy abandoned by his friends, he declares his entry into "a creaturehood of a more advanced order," he describes himself as a "young animal confounded—solitary, furious, eccentric, growing bold."[7] This "young animal"—the phrase reflects Quinn's essential freedom from a socially determined past—becomes a rebel with too many causes: Quinn will oppose war, racism, class oppression, secret societies, condescending WASPs. These are good, liberal oppositions, but they do not comprise a character; lacking a past and making no personal affirmations other than his eccentric commitment to the imagination and to Maud, Quinn seems to possess no moral center.

Daniel Quinn's choices and views may lack a firm basis in character, but the action of the novel is located unambiguously in space and time. Its four sections are subtitled "Albany Winter and Spring 1849–1950," "Saratoga Spring 1850," "Albany Summer 1864," and "Saratoga August 1864." Yet these precise locations serve as the stages for an enormous variety of action. The plot of the novel defies synopsis. As the title indicates, the book belongs to Daniel Quinn. He narrates most of action (though they concentrate on Quinn's experience, the middle two sections are narrated in the third person, and do report some events not witnessed by Quinn), and his life is the novel's central subject matter. The first two sections relate the chaos of experiences which lead the fifteen-year-old Quinn to dedicate himself to his two missions: to claim Maud Fallon as his mate and to become a writer. The last two describe his success, fourteen years later, in achieving both of these goals. But the narrative is not interested in the subtle processes by which a person evolves a sense of himself through interaction with his environment. The environment of *Quinn's Book* is characterized by extreme circumstances which provide the hero with graphic lessons in the ways of the American world in the 1850s and 1860s.

Daniel Quinn is nearly fifteen years old as the novel opens in December 1849. He had come to Albany from Ireland with his parents and sister; in the summer of 1847 they had all died in a cholera epidemic. He has since been working for boatmen on the Erie Canal. The action of the novel opens with flood and fire, death and resurrection. Quinn's early response to these events is justified: "I was bewildered. Nothing seemed to conclude. I was in the midst of a whirlwind panorama of violence and mystery, of tragedy and divine frenzy that mocked every effort at coherence" (57). The whirlwind panorama persists throughout the remaining four-fifths of the narrative. The range of events can be suggested by sketching the lives of some of the principal characters who surround Daniel Quinn.

John (the Brawn) McGee, Quinn's master as the novel opens, works as a boatman on the Erie Canal. As the result of his courageous intervention when her skiff capsizes, he becomes the escort of Magdalena Colón, the notorious dancer and courtesan. After he happens to knock down a famous boxer, he takes up a career in the ring, eventually defeating the American champion. He retires to New York City, where his strong-arm support of the Democratic machine earns him the protection to operate a large, prosperous gambling establishment, and eventually he returns to Saratoga as a major investor in the new racetrack. There is, in fact, a historical model for this implausible career: James Morrisey, the Irish-American heavyweight who won a famous match in 1853 and went on to prosper as a gambler, saloon keeper, labor leader, Congressional representative, and Saratoga racetrack millionaire.[8] Nonetheless, John the Brawn's progress from boatman to millionaire has about it more the quality of operatic exaggeration than of naturalistic probability.

Magdalena Colón, the first of the two female protagonists, also experiences remarkable events. She too seems to have a remarkable historical prototype: Lola Montez (1818–61), the Irish adventuress, dancer, actress, performer of the famous Spider Dance (also Magdalena's speciality), spiritualist, and, as of 1859, religious convert and recluse. Magdalena was born in Ireland. Much-traveled and much-married, she took custody of her twin sister Charlotte's daughter, Maud. It is Charlotte who apparently emulates Lola Montez's dalliance with Ludwig I of Bavaria (see *Quinn's Book* 168); Magdalena's adoption of Maud may constitute a slight parallel to Lola Montez's tutelage of the elfin child actress, Charlotte "Lotta" Crabtree (1847–1924). Magdalena and Maud eventually flee from Spain to America. As the novel opens, Magdalena is drowned while attempting to cross the frozen Hudson River. Hers is the corpse which undergoes a revival as John the Brawn performs a necrophiliac act upon it. She then continues her risqué public performances until she retires to marry the wealthy, slightly degenerate manufacturer Obadiah Griswold. Her niece, Maud, now twelve years old, had accompanied her on the ill-timed river crossing. As John rescues Magdalena, young Daniel Quinn rescues Maud (cold, but completely alive) from the river, and the two children quickly bond to one another. They are forcefully separated when John and Magdalena abandon Daniel, but Quinn takes seriously the promise to steal her which Maud extracted from him. Their relationship remains equivocal, however, and as Daniel spends the 1850s learning his craft as a journalist, Maud pursues a stage career as a dancer, a spirit-rapper, and a nearly nude impersonator of Byron's Mazeppa. Eventually, on the novel's final page, she admits Daniel as her seventh, and presumably final, lover.

If the novel has a main action, it revolves around Quinn's relationship with Maud, and John the Brawn and Magdalena are the more or less conscious sponsors of the affair. The catastrophe which opens the novel brings the four characters together; John and Magdalena are instrumental in dividing the lovers; and Magdalena's elaborate farewell to the world in 1864, organized by John, becomes the occasion for the final reunion of Daniel and Maud. But the extravagant variety of their individual lives prevents any of them from being the mere servants of a romance. Neither John's careers as boxer and gambler nor Magdalena's resurrection and her affair with Obadiah Griswold seem of much relevance to Daniel and Maud. Maud's independence of mind, often whimsical, *is* relevant—it argues that she is no swooning, love-smitten maiden—but her conversations with the spirit world and her career as a performer have no connection with the love plot and so further tend to prevent her relationship with Quinn from providing the novel with a coherent center.

And although one of his two choices—the one depicted in most detail in the narrative—is to dedicate himself to the "romantic quest" (131) of claiming Maud, Quinn is no more preoccupied with Maud than she with him. As the narrator of much of the novel, he has several opportunities to declare his feelings for Maud, but these declarations never carry the force of passion. Quinn is essentially an observer of life, and he tends to observe the peculiar progress of his attraction to Maud with the same detachment that he applies to the other spectacles of his life. Whether he is recounting the bewitchments of Maud or the brutalities of a Civil War battlefield, he resorts to a rhetorical style that expresses a posture—he finds Maud to be baffling and fascinating, war to be dirty and ironic—but precludes either analysis or sincere emotion. He is neither a thinker nor a feeler. He is an observer.

And the novel gives him much to observe. His observations of slavery may serve as representative. Slavery is not an inevitable topic for an Albanian, but, as Kennedy notes in *O Albany!* slaves could be found in Albany as early as 1650. By 1827 slavery had been abolished in New York, and Albany was a station on the Underground Railroad.[8] Quinn first encounters the problem when an escaped slave, Joshua, is discovered in hiding. Quinn instinctively supports his friends—a crude canaler, a liberal newspaper editor, a patrician Dutch widow, a twelve-year old girl—in their unanimous, spontaneous resolve to aid the slave. Joshua eventually becomes John the Brawn's lieutenant, working in his corner of the boxing ring and later dealing cards in his gambling den. Joshua also works mightily for the Underground Railroad, once soliciting Quinn's willing assistance in trapping two slave hunters. In the end Joshua is lynched in a New York City antidraft riot (the historical riot took place in July 1863). Quinn reports these events; he has no need to analyze them. Not only is everyone (except the two miserable slave hunters) opposed to slavery; everyone (quite improbably) respects the human dignity of African-Americans. John the Brawn has only once to be warned (by twelve-year-old Maud) not to use the word "nigger." Quinn does not need to compose an attitude toward slavery; his compassion is instantaneous and complete; it requires no evolution. He can simply assert Joshua's nobility; he need not present Joshua as a human character. The melodrama of Joshua's life constitutes a didactic lesson (and, in the novel, an uncontroversial one), not a biography.

Similarly, the fates of the other secondary characters of the novel represent discrete spectacles, presented as lessons rather than as lives with which Quinn is humanly engaged. Several are presented as genealogical phenomena—the Staats, the Fitzgibbons, the Plums. The Staats represent the expiring old order. Kennedy had acknowledged the priority of the Dutch in Albany by devoting the second chapter of *O Albany!* to Huybertie Pruyn, a Dutch dowager born in 1853 of a family who had arrived in Albany by 1646. Hillegond Staats occupies a similar position in *Quinn's Book*. Though she herself is the daughter of a Dutch tavern-keeper, Kennedy provides an eight-page summary of seven generations of the Staats family into which she has married: Wouter Staats, who arrived in Albany in 1638; his son Johannes; grandson Dolph; great-grandson Jacobus (who, by taking an Indian paramour, briefly brings Native Americans into the narrative); great-great-grandson Volkert; and his great-great-great-grandson Petrus, who married Hillegond. (There was an actual Staats family which figured prominently in early Albany history; its patriarch, Major Abraham Staats, arrived in 1642. Actual Rosebooms had also been recorded in Albany since 1674.)

Hillegond is a widow, estranged from her only son, Dirck, as the novel opens. Living alone with her servants in the Staats mansion, she readily offers refuge to John, Daniel, Maud, and the apparently dead Magdalena. When the others abandon Daniel, Hillegond takes him in. During Daniel's absence she evidently has a flirtation with Joseph Moran, a singer whom Daniel had known. When Quinn returns in 1864, he learns that Hillegond had been murdered six months previously by, as it is soon revealed, Moran (whose fate is then sealed when a pair of improbable owls attack him with their talons). The Staats mansions had been purchased by wealthy Gordon Fitzgibbon, who happens to be wooing Maud. Fitzgibbon has undertaken expensive redecorations; his own "enormous portrait" hangs where once those of generations of Staats had hung.

Hillegond is not a plausible mid-century Dutch dowager. Rather, she is an emblem of aristocratic elegance, hauteur, and noblesse oblige. Her extinction signifies the extinction of that old order; Gordon Fitzgibbon, his fortune based on his father's iron foundry, represents the new order. This historical transition had already been figured early in the novel when the perfectly preserved corpse of Amos Staats, son of Jacobus and his Indian lover, and a martyr of the American Revolution, exploded into dust in front of Daniel and Maud. That the dust settles on the two children may be a metaphor for the influence of the past, but in fact the two do not even let it interrupt their kiss. The past seems easy enough to shake off in *Quinn's Book*.

Lyman Fitzgibbon, Gordon's father, had appeared in the first part of the novel. He is the capitalist, the founder of the new order, who begins as Petrus Staats's partner in the iron foundry and ends as the possessor of the Staats estate. His son plans an entry into national politics. Gordon, with his confident designs upon Maud, represents the smug new WASP power of wealth and respectability, as opposed to the cleverness of Maud and the moral earnestness of Quinn. (In her treatment of Magdalena and Maud, Gordon's supercilious cousin, Phoebe Strong, reiterates the conflict.) The hegemony of the Fitzgibbons in the Albany of 1864 announces the transition to the Gilded Age. It is to the point that Gordon's Democratic opponent may be the Irish former proletarian, John the Brawn. Class antagonisms are more evident in *Quinn's Book* than in any of Kennedy's novels since *The Ink Truck*. The fight between Maud and Phoebe is a comic version of the more tragic violence between the Ryans and the Palmers.

Lyman Fitzgibbon's transitional alliance with Petrus Staats has another consequence: the two are founding members of the secret organization The Society. Dirck Staats, the alienated son of Petrus and Hillegond, works for the newspaper editor Will Canaday and has compiled a coded record of The Society's atrocities. The Society orders Dirck's kidnapping; he is tortured, and his tongue is cut out before he is released to fifteen-year-old Daniel Quinn. Meanwhile Quinn has deciphered Dirck's code, and Will Canaday's paper has published the nefarious actions of The Society, thereby bringing it into disrepute.

The Society finds willing tools in poor whites like the Plums. The Plums are a Snopeslike family who first arrived in Albany in 1759. They—like the Palmers who engage in the bloody confrontation with the Ryans—represent the English proletarians who are easily manipulated into destructive opposition to the later-arriving Irish proletarians like the Quinns and the Ryans and the Daughertys. Young Eli (Peaches) Plum is a bully who threatens Daniel Quinn, but whom Daniel easily outwits. In his lecture on the ugliness of war, Quinn relates Peaches's ultimate pathetic fate: after several times selling his services as a substitute for a drafted middle-class son, he was finally inducted into the Union army. Captured after attempting to desert, he was executed.

Two other characters play important roles in Daniel Quinn's life, both as surrogates for his absent father. One is Emmett Daugherty, who took care of Daniel when his parents and his sister died of cholera. Having saved the life of Lyman Fitzgibbon, Emmett rises to a supervisory position in the iron foundry. Intelligent and working-class, he remains a strong father figure and refuge for Daniel. When, at the end of the long first section, Daniel declares the end of his own childhood and sets out on his missions to claim Maud and become a writer, Emmett escorts him out of Albany, taking him first to view the "Irish circus." This proves to be the spectacle of the "troubled throng" of Irish immigrants passing through Albany on their way west. Emmett's "missionary" concern for these masses affects Daniel; Daugherty serves as Daniel's Irish conscience.

The second important character, Will Canaday, serves as Daniel's writer's conscience. Fifty years old, Canaday is the founder and editor of the *Albany Chronicle*. He is a good, liberal man who crusades against secret societies and slavery. He immediately recognizes young Daniel's worth, takes him on as an apprentice journalist, and, when Daniel leaves Albany, provides him with references and a secure market for his articles. Neither surrogate father really engages in an intimate relationship with Quinn; Daniel uses them in the best sense, but he does not need them the way Billy Phelan needs Francis or Martin Daugherty needs Edward.

Quinn's vocation—journalism—is not, of course, surprising. Bailey and Martin Daugherty have preceded him as journalist heroes. The type has an obvious appeal to William Kennedy, the Albany journalist. But perhaps the most interesting aspect of *Quinn's Book* emerges in connection with the calling of its hero. All three journalist heroes are good men who seek to use their podium to liberate their readers. Bailey's absurdities are an attempt to dissolve the banal prejudices of his moribund audience. The given example of Martin Daugherty's journalism is his appeal to free Billy Phelan from the unjust decree of the McCall political machine. And Daniel Quinn devotes himself to recording the pointless suffering of slaves and soldiers.

But the three heroes are not equally successful. Martin, the decent man with a limited ambition, succeeds: Billy is restored to his world. And Martin will continue in his uneasy compromise with the McCall machine, at times censoring himself, at times speaking out. Bailey and Daniel Quinn are much more ambitious and much less successful. Bailey loses the strike; at the end of the novel he is reduced to uttering answerless riddles. Quinn does not end slavery or warfare. As he lectures an Albany audience on the gross realities of war, Quinn watches his offended audience disperse. Kennedy's first and fifth novels share many qualities; an important one is that both seem to imply the failure of the advocate journalist.

Quinn's Book examines more than the inadequacy of advocacy journalism. One of the distinctive features of the middle Albany novels—*Legs, Billy Phelan's Greatest Game,* and *Ironweed*—is the elliptical, colloquial style with which the characters speak. They do not need to complete sentences or thoughts in order to communicate with their fellow gangsters, players, or bums. Martin Daugherty speaks the same language as Patsy McCall, Billy Phelan, and guys like Footers O'Brien and Lemon Lewis. And so, when Martin writes about Billy's situation, everyone in Billy's Albany understands. And if Martin slips in an alien notion—such as referring to Billy as a magician—the phrase is immediately seized upon and used as a tag by Footers and Lemon to identify Billy.

Quinn's Book is an anthology of modes of oral and written communication. Characters speak or write (or sing) to other individuals, to mass audiences, even to the missing and the dead. Only the singers like Heidi Grahn and Joseph K. Moran have much success, but then their goal is expression, not communication. They may move their auditors, but none of them pretends to transmit a specific message. Attempts of the latter sort—attempts to communicate a particular message through supernatural or natural means—enjoy only questionable success in *Quinn's Book*.

All of Kennedy's protagonists have been the recipients of mystical communications: Bailey's visions, Jack Diamond's talk with the birdman, Martin Daughtery's precognitions, Francis Phelan's ghosts. But not even *The Ink*

Truck was as permeated with supernatural events and messages as is *Quinn's Book*. These begin dramatically with the opening episode of Magdalena's apparent death and resurrection. She reports a vision of being welcomed to the cozy, well-lit river bottom by a pretty doll-child in a gingham dress.

Maud has several encounters with a spirit who shakes a theater and later joins in a séance. There is a historical source for this melodramatic development. The nineteenth-century vogue of spirit-rapping did begin in March 1848 in New York (somewhat west of Albany, however) when two young sisters, Katherine and Margaretta Fox, suddenly began to receive rapping messages from the dead. Though celebrated on both sides of the Atlantic, the Foxes eventually confessed to a hoax.[9] Maud's rapping spirit is apparently genuine, but her dialogues with him seem inconclusive. She forces him to admit he was a person involved in one of her visions, an emaciated man who may have killed the woman he loved. The vision and the dialogue are clearly connected to the love theme which runs through the novel, but the nature of the connection remains obscure. The dead who haunted Francis Phelan were the dead of his own past; the dead of *Quinn's Book* are not Quinn's (or Maud's) dead. The rapping spirit's motives are as confused as his message.

Some of the visions and dreams in the novel are spontaneous; others are solicited through mesmerism, séances, and rituals, but they are often inconclusive. When Hillegond employs the services of Maximilian, the "world-renowned phrenomagnetist," her trance yields a vivid but useless vision of the captivity of her son (79). Maud performs the elaborate Gypsy ritual of baking a "dumb cake" in order to discover who her husband will be, but the result is not revealed (172–3). Previously Maud has had a bizarre dream about "a living, pulsating, disembodied eye" (171). She herself interprets it "as an omen of confusion, especially in regard to Quinn," and the confusion is never clarified.

Other visions do prove exactly prophetic. Daniel Quinn looks into the eyeball of the apparently dead Magdalena and has three successive visions: of "a procession of solemn pilgrims," of a mob of men smashing a newspaper office, of a young man being abducted (17–18). The first of these is verified as Will Canaday leads John, Hillegond, Maud, and Daniel to the mausoleum where the badly wounded slave, Joshua, is chained to the dead prisoner. This, Quinn explicitly observes, is "the same procession of pilgrims I had witnessed in the once-dead eyeball of Magdalena Colón" (37). The stoning of Canaday's newspaper office occurs twice during the turmoil over his exposé of The Society. The abduction is certainly that of Dirck Staats. Hillegond Staats's recurring nightmare—"that should she ever consider a man as a second spouse, he would strangle her in her bed with a ligature" (28)—is fulfilled fifteen years later when Joseph Moran does strangle her in her bed after she does briefly consider marrying him.

The ambivalence of supernatural messages is embodied most importantly in the disk bequeathed to Daniel by his father. It is Daniel's only inheritance, his only direct link to his Irish past. Concealed in the bottom of an old birdcage, it is "a circular metal disk bearing an odd trompe l'oeil design. Now it was a screaming mouth with vicious eyes, now a comic puppy with bulbous nose and tiny mouth" (73). A drawing of it (Kennedy confirms that it represents an actual Celtic disk discovered by archaeologists) appears on the novel's title page. Quinn never deciphers its meaning. His first thought is that it is a potato platter. Will Canaday guesses it is a Roman or Viking bronze; Quinn later refers to it as a Celtic artifact. It certainly functions as an emblem of continuity in Quinn's life, but its provenance and significance remain enigmatic.

More mundane modes of communication also prove of questionable utility in *Quinn's Book*. Quinn's speech on war to his vanishing Albany audience illustrates the problem. There are a large number of writers in the novel. Some write for a public: Quinn, the journalist; Will Canaday, the editor; Gordon Fitzgibbon, who has translated Virgil; Amos Staats, the half-Indian, who began a history of the Staats. Others write in distinctly private veins; Dirck Staats, who writes about The Society in a secret language; Magdalena, who writes cryptic poems; Maud, who, at age four, filled notebooks with an incomprehensible poetic language. But if there are many writers, there are few readers, and they do not understand. Quinn is baffled by Magdalena's poetry; Maud's parents are baffled by hers.

Maud writes a long letter to Quinn explaining her feelings for him, but because he feels alienated by her profitable exhibitions of herself, he does not read the letter until six years after it was written. Quinn does not write letters to Maud, but a large section of his autobiographical narrative in the first section presents itself as a psychic epistle to the absent Maud. There is no indication that Maud receives the message.

The inadequacy of language is most graphically exemplified in the figure of Dirck Staats. Dirck identifies himself as "a devotee of words" (51), but he compiles his history of The Society (itself defined by secret rituals and codes) in a private language composed of "ancient Teutonic runes and Hebrew and Arabic characters" (88) in order to prevent anyone from understanding it. His last cry as he is being abducted is "Save my book." Quinn does, and eventually decodes its account of The Society. Published in Canaday's *Chronicle,* the account leads to embarrassment, suicide, and death for members of The Society, and to this extent language—deciphered—seems to be power. But The Society is not dissolved; Lyman Fitzgibbon, a founder, is almost ready to repudiate it, but other events interrupt his renunciation, and The Society presumably remains a secret force in social affairs. The Society does not kill Dirck, but it does have his tongue torn out, and he is reduced to scribbling messages on paper for Daniel to read. That the inarticulate Dirck finally marries a Swedish singer and moves to Sweden makes for an ironic end. The young man who aimed to alter his world with words ends in a foreign land as the silent adorer of an expressive singer.

Quinn the journalist transcribes the slave stories he hears from Joshua, but he eventually realizes the vanity of his effort. "All that I had written for Will and for the *Tribune* seemed true enough, but a shallow sort of truth. . . . Joshua's life, or John's, or my own could only be hinted at by the use of the word as I had been practicing it" (265). Quinn's first great discovery had been the power of words: he chose to be a writer because "paragraphs are also real in their way. I've seen how they can change things" (146). When he composes his first sentence, he "understands that he has just changed his life" (170). But in the end he is disillusioned about the power of writing. "The magnificent, which is to say the tragic or comic crosscurrents and complexities of such lives, lay somewhere beyond the limits of my calling. . . . I was in need of freedom from inhibition, from dead language, from the repetitions of convention'' (265). A bum like Francis Phelan was able to use the limited resources of his proletarian language to comprehend and to communicate the crosscurrents of his dramatic experience, but for Daniel Quinn, the writer, life exceeds language.

Quinn's crisis may reflect his author's own reevaluation of the medium of his art. The epigraph to Book One is taken from Camus: '' . . . a man's work is nothing but this slow trek to rediscover, through the detours of art, those two or three great and simple images in whose presence his heart first opened.'' The novel's exploration of the roots of the Albany/Irish-American experience may represent a step in Kennedy's trek to rediscover significant images from his past, images which can serve as the basis for the development of his artistic vision. More specifically, the extravagances of *Quinn's Book* may derive from Kennedy's ambition to emulate Daniel Quinn: to free *his* imagination in order to capture ''the magnificent'' in *his* fiction. If the fantastic action and rhetorical excesses of *The Ink Truck* are, in part, Kennedy's response to the social turmoil of the 1960s, the similar action and excesses of *Quinn's Book* may be, in part, a response to Kennedy's experience of the 1980s. Facile analyses serve little purpose, but surely the events of the Reagan years and Kennedy's exposure to the media after *Ironweed*'s dramatic debut in 1983 must have affected his approach to literature. In his middle three novels Kennedy set himself the task of recovering the accessible past, and he produced a coherent portrait of Albany in the 1930s. In his first and most recent novels his projects have been quite different: in the one he draws a comic cartoon of the present; in the other he sketches historical scenes from the past. In both he aims at a more uninhibited narrative, a narrative characterized by imaginative freedom. And this would seem to answer precisely to Quinn's sense that his world has exceeded the grasp of his language, that "inhibition," "dead language," "repetitions of convention" are constraining him and preventing him from fully realizing himself as an artist.

Quinn's conclusion is that "only intuitions culled from an anarchic faith in unlikely gods could offer me an answer" (266). The novel, however, grants him no opportunity to cull intuitions. It moves quickly to its end by turning from the writer theme to the romance theme; Quinn's union with Maud. So, just as Quinn's pursuit of Maud (and the novel itself) ends the moment before its consummation, Quinn's pursuit of the word ends just as he completes his apprenticeship as a writer. The novel concludes on the verge of new beginnings. Quinn's pursuit of a location ends with him arriving at points of departure.

And so, perhaps, the novel is not really pessimistic about the possibilities of changing the world through words. Toward the end of the novel Quinn walks through the Albany Bazaar. His attention is drawn to a manuscript—"handwritten words in a locked cabinet." A card identifies the document: "Original Draft of the President's First Emancipation Proclamation dated September 22, 1862" (215). The draft is being raffled off, and Quinn purchases a ticket. Lincoln's Proclamation altered history; its words did make people free.

Quinn's Book does not conclude William Kennedy's Albany cycle. Although it is the third novel in the Phelan-Quinn-Daugherty saga, it actually represents a deliberate attempt to *begin* the cycle. That is, after completing *Ironweed*, Kennedy saw the necessity of establishing the roots of his families and of his city. And in addition to setting out the historical antecedents of his people and his place, Kennedy also sounds the first notes of particular thematic motifs which he has pursued (or intends in the future to pursue) in novels set in later times: romantic love, social class, race, journalism, theater and theatricality, Irishness.

His next novel will thus, in a sense, justify *Quinn's Book;* it will play out developments based on those themes announced in *Quinn's Book.* Kennedy has described his work in progress as a novel set in 1958, "though it covers events in 1951–52 in Germany and goes backward into the '40s, mid-30s, turn of the century and so on." It will focus primarily upon the Phelans, "but the principal characters have not been written about before."[10] He has also suggested that it might take shape as "a potential sequel to *Quinn's;* it's a potential antecedent for *Billy Phelan's Greatest Game*—the Daugherty family, *The Flaming Corsage* novel."[11] *The Flaming Corsage* is the title of the play (mentioned in *Billy Phelan's Greatest Game*) which Edward Daugherty, Martin's father, wrote in 1908–09 about his scandalous relationship with his wife and his mistress. The two plans are not inconsistent; having set down the roots of his world in *Quinn's Book* and drawn some major branches in *Billy Phelan's Greatest Game* and *Ironweed,* Kennedy is now free to range through the centuries, even in a single novel. His announced intention to do so in what became *Quinn's Book* was frustrated by the need to fix those roots. Now, having placed these themes in his fictional world, Kennedy may amplify upon them in various directions, using various characters.

An intimation of how Kennedy may exploit the materials he has laid out in his Albany novels, especially *Quinn's Book,* may be obtained by briefly looking at his short stories. To date, the Albany cycle includes only two short stories. Though he began his career as an imaginative writer in the genre, his work in the short story has been, in his own judgment, less successful. "I wrote a lot of short stories that didn't go anywhere, and after a while, I gave up."[12] Two early short stories were published in *The San Juan Review:* "The Concept of Being Twenty-Two" (1964), about two American couples who spend a weekend in Puerto Rico, and "Figgy Blue" (1966), about an educated ex-truck driver who feels dislocated when he moves to Puerto Rico. Kennedy describes these as "some short stories set in Puerto Rico with the beginnings of political contexts, but they were shallow, and I realized it was because I didn't know very much about the place."[13]

Although excerpts from his novels have been published in *Epoch, Esquire,* and *Harper's,* Kennedy has published only two short stories since the 1960s. In 1983 the short story "The Secrets of Creative Love" appeared in *Harper's.* And in 1985 he revised an old story for publication in the *Glens Falls Review* as "An Exchange of Gifts." Both of these are linked to the Phelan-Daugherty-Quinn saga ("The Secrets of Creative Love" even offers the incidental revelation that the Daniel Quinn of *Quinn's Book* "was shot in a love duel."[14]); both were written at a time when Kennedy's plan for *Quinn's Book* reportedly included alternating nineteenth- and twentieth-century chapters. Both present excerpts from the life of the twentieth-century Daniel Quinn who appeared as a ten-year-old in *Billy Phelan's Greatest Game* and *Ironweed,* and in both there are references to Quinn's experiences in Germany—experiences which, at one stage, were apparently intended as part of the novel which became *Quinn's Book*.

"An Exchange of Gifts" is the slighter effort: it is a brief sketch set in the 1950s in which Daniel Quinn returns to his North Albany neighborhood from Germany and attempts to help a mother and a sister confront the fate of a son and brother who was shot down in Korea and has been recorded as missing in action, presumed dead. Only three pages long, "An Exchange of Gifts" reveals very little about Daniel Quinn, but it deals suggestively and effectively with a complex set of relationships. The sister puts on an old dress, and for a few moments she and Quinn dance, reenacting their past. This echoes other such moments in Kennedy's fiction: Francis Phelan recovering his past by dressing in his 1916 suit in *Ironweed,* or, more substantially, Martin Daugherty and Melissa Spencer briefly resuming their affair in *Billy Phelan's Greatest Game,* or Quinn and Sissy Pennington briefly resuming an affair in "The Secrets of Creative Love." The past is inescapable but never entirely unreconstitutable in the world of Kennedy's fiction.

"The Secrets of Creative Love" is a more revealing story, and it may serve as an indication of the future direction of Kennedy's fiction. Though it antedates *Quinn's Book,* it acquired its full resonance only after the appearance of the novel. The story's twentieth-century Daniel Quinn is, like his nineteenth-century ancestor in the novel, married to a Maud (the rules of consanguinity would suggest that this Maud cannot, however, claim the novel's Maud as *her* ancestor). And the penultimate sentence of the story—"Maud rolled backward onto the simple iron bed, her legs rising, the ribbon falling naturally between her open thighs, leaving her gift mostly secret"[15]—is identical to the antepenultimate sentence of the novel. This set of doubled couples and doubled endings is not, as it might seem, the result of a discarded stage in the composition of the novel. Kennedy has been definite on the subject: the story is "a moment in the lives of the contemporary Quinn and Maud," one "upon which I may elaborate at some point in the future."[16]

The story is, then, a model of the sort of fiction which Kennedy is now free to compose. It extracts a moment in an already adumbrated continuum between the 1850s and the 1950s, a continuum of family and city history. And it plays a variation upon an already announced theme. In this instance the theme is that of romantic love—the nineteenth-century love of Daniel Quinn and Maud Fallon. "The Secrets of Creative Love" recounts how the twentieth-century Daniel and Maud visit the wealthy Pennington's of Saratoga—Fred, Daniel's old journalist friend, and Sissy, Maud's cousin. This Daniel Quinn was born in the same year as his author and has followed in his author's footsteps: college, newspaper reporting, a career as a writer. He is another of Kennedy's journalist heroes (thus striking, very slightly and only incidentally, the journalism theme; Fred Pennington is also a journalist-editor). One evening, at a lakeside party, Quinn observes Maud depart on a boat ride with Fred. He and Sissy then decide to reprise an old affair. Maud returns, and the story ends the way (and in the words) that *Quinn's Book* ended: with a Daniel Quinn about to make love to a Maud. The complete significance of these echoes will emerge when Kennedy provides a fuller account of the characters of the twentieth-century Daniel and Maud in his next novel.

The story depicts a variety of love relationships: open (Daniel and Maud); occasional (Daniel and Sissy); possessive (Cesar, a uxorious Dominican horsebreeder, and his wife, Carmen). Cesar (seriously) and Daniel (playfully) both suggest that if Fred Pennington has seduced their wives, justice requires Sissy Pennington to acquiesce in a compensatory seduction. She does, in fact, briefly renew an old affair with Daniel, but as much on her initiative as his. It is, however, in his relationship with Maud that Daniel achieves creative love. The secret of this love would seem to be contained in the peculiar dream Maud relates to Daniel. But like all mystical moments in Kennedy's fiction, its exact meaning remains uncertain.

The characters and themes of Kennedy's next novel will surely be drawn from those already established in the Albany cycle. How they will be developed—what parallels and echoes will emerge—remains uncertain, but whatever its focus, the novel will further define Albany as a place "centered squarely in the American and human continuum," a concrete location for William Kennedy's fictional exploration of the experience of his dislocated heroes.

NOTES

1. Edward C. Reilly, "On an Averill Park Afternoon with William Kennedy; *The South Carolina Review* 21 (1989): 18.

2. Reilly 18.

3. Alvin P. Sanoff, "A Novelist's Need to Go Home Again," *U.S. News and World Report* 20 June 1988:66.

4. Sanoff 66.

5. T. Coraghessan Boyle, "Into the Heart of Old Albany," *The New York Times Book Review* 22 May 1988:32.

6. See, e.g., John Chute, *Times Literary Supplement* 17 June 1988: 680; Richard Eder, *Los Angeles Times Book Review* 22 May 1988: 3; Stephen Wall, *London Review of Books* 1 Sept. 1988: 21; Christopher Lehmann-Haupt, *The New York Times* 16 May 1988: C18.

Quinn's Book

7. William Kennedy, *Quinn's Book* (New York: Viking, 1988) 61. Subsequent references will be noted in parentheses.

8. Edward C. Reilly, "John the Brawn McGee in *Quinn's Book:* A Probable Source," *Notes on Contemporary Literature* 19 (1989): 4–5.

9. Ruth Brandon, *The Spiritualists* (New York: Knopf, 1983) 1–42.

10. Personal letter to the author, 9 Feb. 1990.

11. Reilly, "On an Averill Park Afternoon" 23–24.

12. Reilly, "On an Averill Park Afternoon" 19.

13. Larry McCaffery and Sinda Gregory, "An Interview with William Kennedy," *Alive and Writing* (Urbana: University of Illinois Press, 1987) 154–55.

14. William Kennedy, "The Secrets of Creative Love," *Harper's* July 1983:58.

15. Kennedy, "The Secrets of Creative Love," 58.

16. William Kennedy, Personal letter to the author, 23 Jan. 1990.

Genealogy of the Phelans and the Quinns

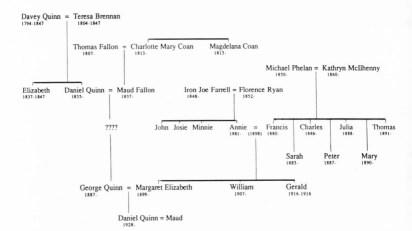

NOTE:

Most of the information in appendixes 1 and 2 can be verified by a careful reading of the three novels: *Billy Phelan's Greatest Game, Ironweed,* and *Quinn's Book.* However, some of the names and dates were supplied directly by William Kennedy. For his kindness in this and other matters, I am grateful.

Quinn-Phelan-Daugherty Chronology

1813	Magdelana and Charlotte Mary Coan born in Ireland
1835	Daniel Quinn born to Davey Quinn and Teresa Brennan
1837	Maud Lucinda Fallon born to Thomas Fallon and Charlotte Mary Coan
ca. 1840	Emmett Daugherty emigrates from Ireland to New York with brother Owen
1847	Daniel Quinn's father, mother, and sister die of cholera
1849	Magdalena Coan Colon and Maud Fallon come to the United States; Daniel Quinn rescues Maud
1862	Daniel Quinn reports from Civil War battlefields
1864	Daniel Quinn "steals" Maud Fallon
1880	Francis Aloysius born to Michael and Kathryn Phelan
1887	(Helen Marie born to Brian and Mary J. N. Archer) George Quinn born
1888	Martin Daugherty born
1897	Francis's affair with Katrina Daugherty
1899	Margaret born to Francis and Annie Farrell Phelan
1901	Francis kills Harold Allen with a stone; plays baseball for Dayton
1902	Edward Daugherty's play, *The Car Barns*, based on Francis's stone-throwing

Appendix 2

1907	Billy Phelan born to Francis and Annie Phelan
1908	Edward Daugherty–Melissa Spencer love nest
1912	Katrina Daugherty dies in a fire
1916	Gerald Michael Phelan born, dies; Francis departs Albany
1919	Patsy McCall's first political victory
1920	Martin Daugherty marries Maire (Mary) Kiley
1924	Peter born to Martin and Mary Daugherty
1928	Daniel born to George and Margaret Phelan Quinn; Martin Daugherty's "debauch" with Melissa Spencer
1929	Francis Phelan meets Helen Archer; Helen suffers a miscarriage
1930	Francis kills Rowdy Dick, loses fingertip
1931	(Jack "Legs" Diamond killed)
1934	Francis returns to Albany for his mother's funeral
1938	Charlie Boy McCall abducted; Martin Daugherty's second debauch with Melissa Spencer; Francis and Helen return to Albany; Francis meets Billy and returns home; Helen dies

BIBLIOGRAPHY

Books by William Kennedy

NOVELS

The Ink Truck. New York: Dial, 1969 (Viking, 1984); London: Macdonald, 1970.

Legs. New York: Coward, McCann, 1975 (Penguin, 1983); London: Cape, 1977.

Billy Phelan's Greatest Game. New York: Viking, 1978 (Penguin, 1983); London: Penguin, 1984.

Ironweed. New York: Viking, 1983; Harmondsworth: Penguin, 1984.

Quinn's Book. New York: Viking, 1988; London: Cape, 1988.

CHILDREN'S FICTION

Charlie Malarkey and the Belly Button Factory (with Brenden Kennedy). Boston: Atlantic Monthly, 1986; London: Cape, 1987.

NONFICTION

O Albany! Improbable City of Political Wizards, Fearless Ethnics, Spectacular Aristocrats, Splendid Nobodies, and Underrated Scoundrels. New York: Viking; [Albany, NY]: Washington Park Press, 1983.

The Capitol in Albany. New York: Aperature, 1986.

The Making of Ironweed. New York: Penguin, 1988. Originally appeared as "(Re)creating *Ironweed*." *American Film* Jan/Feb 1988: 18–25.

Selected Short Fiction, Screenplays, Essays, and Reviews by Kennedy

SHORT FICTION

"The Concept of Being Twenty-Two." *The San Juan Review* 1 (June 1964): 18–20, 27–29.

"An Exchange of Gifts." *Glens Falls Review* 3 (1985/86): 7–9.

"Figgy Blue." *The San Juan Review* 3 (Feb. 1966): 36–38.

"The Secrets of Creative Love." *Harper's* July 1983: 54–58.

SCREENPLAYS

The Cotton Club (with Francis Ford Coppola), Orion, 1984. New York: St. Martin's Press, 1986.

Ironweed, Tri-Star, 1987.

NONFICTION

"The Yellow Trolley Car in Barcelona and Other Visions: A Profile of Gabriel Garcia Márquez." *Atlantic Monthly* Jan. 1973: 50–59.

"The Lobsterman Who Runs the Assembly." *The New York Times Magazine* 23 Apr. 1973: 12–13, 50, 54, 56, 59–63.

"Rocky Is 64, Going on 35." *New York Times Magazine* 29 Apr. 1973: 16–17, 58, 60, 62, 64, 66–67.

"The Quest for Heliotrope, or, A Week in Dublin with the Curious Verbivorous Joyceans." *Atlantic Monthly* May 1974:53–60.

"Getting It All, Saving It All: Some Notes by an Extremist." New York State Governor's Conference on Libraries, 1978.

"If Saul Bellow Doesn't Have A True Word to Say, He Keeps His Mouth Shut." *Esquire* Feb. 1982: 48–50, 52, 54.

"Everything Everybody Ever Wanted." *Atlantic Monthly* May 1983: 77–84, 87–88. Reprinted as "The South Mall: Everything Everybody Ever Wanted." *O Albany!* 304–24.

"William Kennedy's Cotton Club Stomp." *Vanity Fair* Nov. 1984: 42–48, 116–18.

"How Winning the Pulitzer Has Changed One Writer's Life." *Life* Jan. 1985: 156–8.

"Jack and the Oyster." *Esquire* June 1985: 37–40.

"My Life in the Fast Lane." *Esquire* June 1986: 59–60.

"Be Reasonable—Unless You're a Writer." *The New York Times Book*

Bibliography

Review 25 Jan. 1987: 3. And see "William Kennedy Replies," *The New York Times Book Review* 1 Mar. 1987:35.

"Carlos Fuentes: Dreaming of History." *Review of Contemporary Fiction* 8 (1988): 234–37.

"Why It Took So Long." *The New York Times Book Review* 20 May 1990: 1, 32–35.

SELECTED BOOK REVIEWS

The Lime Works, by Thomas Bernhard, *The New Republic* 15 Dec. 1973:28–30.

One Hundred Years of Solitude, by Gabriel García Márquez. *The National Observer* 20 Apr. 1970: 23.

The Blood Oranges, by John Hawkes. *Look* 5 Oct. 1971: 64.

The Dangerous Summer, by Ernest Hemingway. *The New York Times Book Review* 9 June 1985: 1, 32–33, 35.

Working Days and *The Grapes of Wrath,* by John Steinbeck. *The New York Times Book Review* 9 Apr. 1989: 1, 44–45.

Interviews

Allen, Douglas R., and Mona Simpson. "The Art of Fiction CXI William Kennedy." *The Paris Review* 112 (Winter 1989): 34–59.

Barbato, Joseph. "PW Interviews William Kennedy." *Publishers Weekly* 9 Dec. 1983: 52–53.

Bonetti, Kay. "An Interview with William Kennedy." *The Missouri Review* 8 (1985): 71–86.

Farrelly, Patrick. "Francis Phelan Goes Hollywood." *Irish America* Nov. 1987: 25–29, 51.

McCaffery, Larry, and Sinda Gregory. "An Interview with William Kennedy." *Alive and Writing: Interviews with American Writers of the 1980s.* Urbana: University of Illinois Press, 1987. 151–74. Originally appeared in *Fiction International* 15 (1984): 157–79.

Quinn, Peter J. "William Kennedy: An Interview." *The Recorder: A Journal of the American Irish Historical Society* 1 (1985): 65–81.

Reilly, Edward C. "On an Averill Park Afternoon with William Kennedy." *The South Carolina Review* 21 (1989): 11–24.

Bibliography

Sanoff, Alvin P. "A Novelist's Need to Go Home Again." *U.S. News and World Report* 20 June 1988: 66.

Thomson, David. "The Man Has Legs." *Film Comment* 21 (1985): 54–59.

Bibliography

Reilly, Edward C. "A William Kennedy Bibliography," *Bulletin of Bibliographies* (forthcoming: June 1991).

Critical and Biographical Commentaries on Kennedy

Agrest, Susan. "Tough Guy with a Golden Touch." *Hudson Valley Magazine* July 1987: 42–49, 72.

Black, David. "The Fusion of Past and Present in William Kennedy's *Ironweed*." *Critique* 27 (1986): 177–84. Sees Kennedy using "a Greek concept of time" in *Ironweed* as Francis struggles to "fuse" his past and his present.

Busby, Mark. "William Kennedy." *DLB Yearbook 1985*. Ed. J. W. Ross. Detroit: Gale, 1986. 387–94.

Clarke, Peter P. "Classical Myth in William Kennedy's *Ironweed*." *Critique* 27 (1986): 167–76. Identifies numerous classical archetypes underlying *Ironweed:* Odysseus; Venus and Adonis: Artemis; Aeneas; Harpies, Furies, and Fates.

Cloutier, Candace. "William Kennedy." *Contemporary Authors, New Revision Series.* Vol. 14. Ed. L. Metzger. Detroit: Gale, 1985. 258–61. See also *Contemporary Authors* Vol. 85–88 and *Contemporary Literary Criticism* Vols. 6, 28, 34, 53.

Croyden, Margaret. "The Sudden Fame of William Kennedy." *The New York Times Magazine* 26 Aug. 1984: 33, 43, 52–53, 57, 59, 64, 68, 70, 73.

Gibb, Robert. "The Life of the Soul: William Kennedy, Magical Realist." PhD. diss. Lehigh University, 1986.

Griffin, Paul F. "The Moral Implications of Annie Phelan's Jell-O." *San Jose Studies* 14 (1988): 85–95.

———— . "Susan Sontag, Franny Phelan, and the Moral Implications of Photographs." *Midwest Quarterly* 29 (1987): 194–203. By using a snapshot from an attic trunk as a moral guidepost on his way to recovering his place in his family, Francis undermines Sontag's claim of the essential falseness of photography.

Hunt, George W. "William Kennedy's Albany Trilogy." *America* 19 May 1984: 373–75. Notes liturgical elements in three Albany novels.

————, and Peter Quinn. "William Kennedy's Albany." *America* 17 Mar. 1984: 189–90. Review of *O Albany!*

Johnson, B. R. "William Kennedy." *Beacham's Popular Fiction in America.* Ed. W. Beacham. Washington: Beacham, 1986. 718–25.

King, Anne Mills. "William Kennedy." *Critical Survey of Long Fiction Supplement.* Ed. F. N. Magill. Pasadena: Salem Press, 1987, 193–200.

Murtaugh, Daniel M. "Fathers and Their Sons: William Kennedy's Hero-Transgressors." *Commonweal* 19 May 1989: 298–302. A substantial examination of the important father-son theme in *Billy Phelan's Greatest Game* and *Ironweed;* notes Old Testament elements in the first, New Testament elements in the second.

Nichols, Loxley F. "William Kennedy Comes of Age." *National Review* 9 Aug. 1985: 46–48. A favorable survey of the entire Albany cycle (including *The Ink Truck* and *O Albany!*).

Parini, Jay. "Man of Ironweed." *Horizon* Dec. 1987: 35–36.

Prescott, Peter S. "Having the Time of His Life." *Newsweek* 6 Feb. 1984: 78–79.

Pritchard, William H. "The Spirits of Albany." *The New Republic* 14 Feb. 1983: 37–38. A favorable review of *Ironweed.*

Reilly, Edward C. "Dante's *Purgatorio* and Kennedy's *Ironweed:* Journeys to Redemption." *Notes on Contemporary Literature* 17 (1987): 5–8. Parallels between the two journeys.

———— . "John the Brawn McGee in *Quinn's Book:* A Probable Source." *Notes on Contemporary Literature* 19 (1989): 4–5. Identifies James Morrisey as a prototype for John the Brawn.

———— . "The Pigeons and Circular Flight in Kennedy's Ironweed." *Notes on Contemporary Literature* 2 (1986): 8. Finds an "affirmative vision" in metaphors of flight and circles.

———— . "William Kennedy's Albany Trilogy: Cutting Through the Sludge." *Publications of the Arkansas Philological Association* 12

Bibliography

(1986): 43–55. Views the three novels, *Legs* through *Ironweed,* as a trilogy in which with increasing artistry Kennedy portrays protagonists transcending the "sludge" of life and showing "what a man can do to set things right."

Robertson, Michael. "The Reporter as Novelist: The Case of William Kennedy." *Columbia Journalism Review* 24 (1985–86): 49–52. Biographical survey of Kennedy as journalist/novelist.

Salisbury, Stephan. "William Kennedy's Moveable Feast." *Philadelphia Inquirer Magazine* 31 July 1988: 36–38, 43.

Sheppard, R. Z. "A Winning Rebel with a Lost Cause." *Time,* 1 Oct. 1984: 79–80.

Tierce, Michael. "William Kennedy's Odyssey: The Travels of Francis Phelan." *Classical and Modern Literature* 8 (1988): 247–63. A full treatment of the parallels between *Ironweed* and Homer's *Odyssey.*

Whittaker, Stephen. "The Lawyer as Narrator in William Kennedy's *Legs.*" *Legal Studies Forum* 9 (1985): 157–64. Directs attention toward the complexities of Marcus Gorman's self-serving narration.

Index

139

Index

ACL 6789   3/3/93